# LEARNING AND DEVELOPMENT

## CIPD REVISION GUIDE 2005

**Rosemary Harrison** is the CIPD Chief Examiner for Learning and Development and played a significant role in the development of the latest set of professional standards. She is a leading academic and writer in the field and an established speaker at conferences and universities in the UK and abroad.

The Chartered Institute of Personnel and Development is the leading publisher of books and reports for personnel and training professionals, students, and all those concerned with the effective management and development of people at work. For details of all our titles, please contact the publishing department:

*tel:* 020 8263 3387

*fax:* 020 8263 3850

*e-mail:* publish@cipd.co.uk

The catalogue of all CIPD titles can be viewed on the CIPD website:

www.cipd.co.uk/bookstore

# LEARNING AND DEVELOPMENT

## CIPD REVISION GUIDE 2005

ROSEMARY HARRISON

Chartered Institute of Personnel and Development

Published by the Chartered Institute of Personnel and Development,
CIPD House, Camp Road, London, SW19 4UX

First published 2005

Design and typesetting by Curran Publishing Services, Norwich
Printed in Great Britain by The Cromwell Press, Trowbridge, Wiltshire

British Library Cataloguing in Publication Data
A catalogue record of this revision guide is available from the
British Library

ISBN 1 84398 082 7

The views expressed in this revision guide are the author's own and may
not necessarily reflect those of the CIPD.
    The CIPD has made every effort to trace and acknowledge copyright
holders. If any source has been overlooked, CIPD Enterprises would be
pleased to redress this for future editions.

Chartered Institute of Personnel and Development, CIPD House,
Camp Road, London, SW19 4UX
Tel: 020 8971 9000          Fax: 020 8263 3333
Email: cipd@cipd.co.uk      Website: www.cipd.co.uk
Incorporated by Royal Charter. Registered Charity No. 1079797

# CONTENTS

*Figures and Tables*                                                        *vii*
*Acknowledgements*                                                          *viii*
*Preface*                                                                     *ix*

**Section 1 Introduction to the CIPD's Professional Standards**               **1**
**1  CIPD Professional Standards**                                            **3**
   Introduction                                                                 3
   The CIPD's Professional Development Scheme                                    3
   Advice on tackling the PDS Generalist examinations                           6
   Typical queries from PDS students                                            8
   Conclusion                                                                   11

**Section 2 Revision and examination guidance**                              **13**
**2  Revision and examination guidance**                                     **15**
   Introduction                                                                15
   The CIPD's Learning and Development Generalist Standard                      15
   The Standard's 10 performance indicators and some 'big issues'              17
   Conclusion                                                                   28

**3  Examiner's insights**                                                   **29**
   Introduction                                                                29
   Frequently asked questions about the Learning and Development examination   29
   Conclusion                                                                   38

**Section 3 Examination practice and feedback**                             **39**
**4  Examination questions and feedback**                                   **41**
   Introduction                                                                41
   Reaching Master's-level standard                                            41
   L&D Generalist examination questions and feedback: Section A                43

L&D Generalist examination questions and feedback:
Section B                                                    51
Conclusion                                                  82

**Section 4 Conclusion**                                    **83**
**5 Conclusion**                                            **85**
Using the revision guide                                    85
Doing well on the day                                       85
The experiential learning cycle                            87

**Appendix 1**
Recent CIPD research publications related to the L&D field,
and CIPD research information sources                       89

*References*                                                *93*
*Index*                                                     *97*

# FIGURES AND TABLES

**Figure**

1  The experiential cycle of learning                              88

**Tables**

1  Route map for the *Learning and Development* revision
   guide                                                            x
2  Linking the L&D Standard to the L&D core text                   xii
3  An action-planning template                                    52–3

# ACKNOWLEDGEMENTS

Unless otherwise indicated, comments in this 2005 revision guide are my own and do not represent official views of any other individual or institution.

I acknowledge with thanks the information supplied to me by Linda Emmett, Professional Knowledge Adviser at the CIPD, on the ways in which Professional Development Scheme candidates can update and expand their store of knowledge on research and organisational practice.

My thanks also to my editor Ruth Lake, and to my husband for his usual patient support.

# PREFACE

## The purpose of the revision guides

The purpose of the revision guides is to guide through the CIPD's Professional Development Scheme (PDS) revision and examination processes those of you who are hoping to qualify as CIPD professionals.

Although I use the term 'the L&D examination' as shorthand throughout this *Learning and Development* revision guide, I have written it for all students taking CIPD qualifying examinations in the L&D Generalist field. The advice that it contains is therefore as relevant for part-time as it is for full-time students. It is intended for those who will be internally assessed as well as those who will be taking the CIPD's national examinations.

Of course the guide cannot be a substitute for your core texts and other course materials. It supplements them, and you will find throughout its chapters linkages to wider information sources.

## Structure of the Learning and Development guide

Like all the revision guides this one has four sections, which cover:

1.  Introduction to the CIPD's professional standards

2.  Revision and examination guidance

3.  Examination practice and feedback

4.  Conclusion.

Table 1 will enable you to plan your route through the book.

Those of you who are already familiar with the PDS examinations may wish to simply skim-read Chapter 1 before moving to Chapter 2 as your real starting point. For all of you, Chapter 4 goes to the heart of the matter because it contains a selection of past examination questions

**Table 1** Route map for the *Learning and Development* revision guide

---

### Section 1 Introduction to the CIPD's Professional Standards

**Chapter 1 CIPD Professional Standards**
An introduction to the Standards; preparing for the PDS generalist examinations
Reflections on some FAQs about those examinations

---

### Section 2 Revision and examination guidance

**Chapter 2 Revision and examination guidance**
An explanation of the L&D Standard and the criteria against which L&D candidates are assessed
**Chapter 3 Examiner's insights**
Reflections on some FAQs about the L&D examination

---

### Section 3 Examination practice and feedback

**Chapter 4 Examination questions and feedback**
Guidance on achieving Master's-level performance in the L&D exam
A sample of past L&D examination questions and advice on tackling them

---

### Section 4 Conclusion

**Chapter 5 Conclusion**
Will I pass? Some final advice

that cover the L&D Generalist Standard's 10 knowledge indicators, coupled with advice on how to tackle such questions and examples of candidates' answers to them.

## Information sources

There are many sources of information for you to draw on during your course of study. In addition to the course materials that you will have accumulated there are the CIPD's core text, *Learning and development* (Harrison 2002) and other textbooks on employee development, human resource development and training. There are also the CIPD and other websites.

Feedback on the first edition of this guide, in 2003, indicated a wish for more links to be made to my core text throughout its chapters. I have therefore provided these. Table 2 shows in detail how the text links to the L&D Standard.

Although an important aim of the core text is to help CIPD students who are studying the L&D field, another is to provide a general text that, like its predecessors that I have written since 1988, reaches a wider, non-CIPD market and is informed by many perspectives other than that of the Institute's. In its role as a core CIPD text the book provides full information relating to all areas of the L&D Standard. However its broader purpose is to enhance readers' ability as thinking performers by encouraging a critical approach to all theoretical concepts, models and prescriptions, whatever their source.

It is important to understand, too, that the L&D Generalist Standard's performance indicators (see Chapter 2) do not represent functional tasks. They identify areas of activity to be pursued in an integrative way – that is to say, in a way that takes into account their interactive nature and their links to other human resource areas. Changes made in one area, such as management development, should not be introduced without planning for the related changes that will then be needed in others such as performance management, career management, recruitment, reward and so on. This is why Table 2 does no more than interpret the L&D core text's content in one of many possible ways.

**Table 2** Linking the L&D Standard to the L&D core text

| Performance Indicator and its focus | Indicative content | Chapters containing most relevant material |
|---|---|---|
| 1: Integrating L&D activity into the organisation | 1.1 | 1, 2, 4 and 8 |
| | 1.2 | 3, 4 and 12 |
| | 1.3 | 1, 2, 4, 9 and 12 |
| | 1.4 | 3, 4 and 12 |
| | 1.5 | 4, 5, 9 and 12 |
| 2: Providing a value-adding L&D function | 2.1 | 4, 9, 10, 11, 12 and 14 |
| | 2.2 | 3, 6, 9 and 12 |
| | 2.3 | 8 |
| | 2.4 | 2, 4, 5, 10, 12 and 20 |
| | 2.5 | 5, 11 and 20 |
| | 2.6 | 10 |
| | 2.7 | 3, 4, 5, 6, 9, 12, 14, 15 and 20 |
| 3: Contributing to recruitment and performance management processes | 3.1 | 13 and 17 |
| | 3.2 | 13 |
| | 3.3 | 10 and 13 |
| | 3.4 | 13 and 18 |
| 4: Contributing to employee retention | 4.1 | 17 |
| | 4.2 | 17 |
| | 4.3 | 18 |
| 5: Contributing to building organisational capacity and facilitating change | 5.1 | 3,6 and 19 |
| | 5.2 | 3 and 19 |
| | 5.3 | 3, 17, 18, 19 and 20 |
| | 5.4 | 8, 15, 17, 19 and 20 |
| 6: Stimulating strategic | 6.1 | 18 and 20 |
| | 6.2 | 19 and 20 |

**Table 2** continued

|  | awareness and | 6.3 | 11 and 20 |
|---|---|---|---|
|  | developing | 6.4 | 20 |
|  | knowledge | 6.5 | 11 and 20 |
| 7: | Designing and | 7.1 | 14, 15, 16 and 19 |
|  | delivering | 7.2 | 11 |
|  | learning | 7.3 | 11, 15 and 16 |
|  | processes and | 7.4 | 15, 16 and 19 |
|  | activity |  |  |
| 8: | Evaluating and | 8.1 | 5 and 16 |
|  | assessing L&D | 8.2 | 5 and 16 |
|  | outcomes and | 8.3 | 5 |
|  | investment | 8.4 | 5 and16 |
| 9: | Acting as ethical | 9.1 | 7 |
|  | practitioners | 9.2 | 7 |
|  |  | 9.3 | 7 and 10 |
|  |  | 9.4 | 7 and 10 |
| 10: | Ensuring | 10.1 | 8, 18 and 20 |
|  | continuing | 10.2 | 17 |
|  | professional self- | 10.3 | 9, 13 and 17 |
|  | development | 10.4 | 6 and 20 |
|  |  | 10.5 | 7 and 11 |

Source: Harrison (2002a)

## Achieving Master's-level performance

The CIPD's PDS examinations are officially recognised as being at Master's level. That should not alarm you because the old PQS examinations were set very near that level. As you will find in Chapter 1, the criteria that officially define 'Master's-level' performance are reflected in the PDS in a clear form that links them to the concepts of 'thinking performer' and 'business partner' and to a framework of competencies called 'BACKUP'. The Master's-level nature of the PDS is also reflected in the most visible difference between PQS and PDS examination papers: every PDS paper, regardless of subject, explicitly requires candidates to demonstrate their knowledge of relevant published research and of current widespread organisational practice. Progress here is most promising, with PDS candidates showing an increasing ability to meet this requirement as they become used to incorporating research in their CIPD studies, their coursework and their examination preparation. Appendix 1 lists recent CIPD-sponsored research reports, executive briefings, policy statements and websites relevant to the L&D field to help you here.

I hope that you find this 2005 guide useful as you prepare for your forthcoming examinations. I wish you every success in your future careers as personnel and development professionals.

Rosemary Harrison
Chief examiner: Learning and Development
September 2004

# SECTION 1

## INTRODUCTION TO THE CIPD'S PROFESSIONAL STANDARDS

# I CIPD PROFESSIONAL STANDARDS

## Introduction

This chapter has two aims:

- to introduce the Chartered Institute of Personnel and Development's (CIPD) Professional Development Scheme (PDS) and the core competencies that it targets

- to give some general advice on how to prepare for the PDS examinations and reassure on concerns frequently raised by PDS examination candidates.

The chapter begins with a discussion of concepts and skills that go to the heart of the PDS philosophy. It then outlines the format of PDS Generalist examination papers. It concludes with discussion of some questions often asked by students preparing to take PDS or equivalent examinations.

## The CIPD's Professional Development Scheme

### A Master's-level scheme

The PDS Generalist examinations test candidates against the Institute's new Professional Standards, produced in 2001 after a two-year consultative process. The standards have been extensively communicated to tutors and students, with reminders of key points appearing regularly in, for example, *Shine*, *On Course* and examiners' reports.

The PDS professional qualifications have been identified in the National Qualifications Framework for Higher Education for England, Wales and Northern Ireland as being at Master's level and at the equivalent level in the Scottish framework. A Master's-level performance is officially defined as one that demonstrates:

- a systematic understanding of knowledge and a critical awareness of current problems and/or new insights

- a comprehensive understanding of techniques

- a conceptual understanding that enables the student to evaluate critically both current research and methodologies.

These criteria are reflected in a set of core concepts and competencies that underpin the PDS Standards and the examinations related to them: the *thinking performer*, the *business partner*, and the *BACKUP* framework.

## The thinking performer

*Thinking performers* are knowledgeable and competent in their field, able to move beyond compliance to provide a critique of organisational policies and procedures and advice on how organisations should develop in the future. You can demonstrate competence as a *thinking performer* in your examination answers when you show:

- thinking that is not limited to your organisational level

- understanding of organisation strategy and its context (both internal and external)

- understanding of how to produce plans that will effectively implement strategy at the business unit and operational levels of the organisation

- the capability to evaluate and advise on any wider personnel and development or business implications that your recommendations for action may have, ensuring that they are feasible in the particular organisational context

- knowledge and application of relevant published research, general organisational practice and current thinking.

## The business partner

A *business partner* works with others at his or her level both within and outside the organisation in order to make a strong contribution to organisational performance. You can indicate your ability to act as a business partner when you show in your examination answers that you appreciate the importance of:

- working in collaboration with internal stakeholders in order to achieve P&D goals

- active involvement in external networks in order to increase your knowledge of the general business environment, and to inform and support your professional activity

- keeping fully informed about the P&D implications of internal and external changes affecting the organisation

- raising awareness of key personnel and development (P&D) issues facing the organisation and of their business implications

- continuous data gathering and knowledge sharing to identify and raise awareness of ways in which P&D initiatives are producing, and can produce, added value for the business

- being skilled in managing diversity, and being ethical in all that you do as a P&D professional.

## The BACKUP framework

The *BACKUP* framework highlights five key competencies that reflect the qualities of a thinking performer and business partner:

- *Business orientation*: the ability to focus on the business, its needs and goals, in P&D strategies and their delivery.

- *Application capability*: the ability to apply theory to practical situations, and to produce feasible, value-adding solutions to real-life problems and challenges.

- *Knowledge of the subject matter*: the ability to act in a way that is fully informed, based on a strong and deep base of professional knowledge.

- *Understanding of different organisational scenarios and contexts*: the ability to relate strategies and practices to a variety of different organisational settings, and to ensure that they take full account of the backcloth of vision and goals, management actions, culture and structure that shape people's daily lives in the workplace.

- *Persuasion and presentation skills*: the ability to secure support for P&D proposals through clear, well-structured presentations that use the language of the audience to communicate and gain understanding of their content.

In Chapter 4 I will explain how you can apply these concepts and demonstrate these competencies in the L&D Generalist examination. Here, I want next to offer some general advice about the PDS examinations.

## Advice on tackling the PDS Generalist examinations

### Section A: the case study

In determining how far a candidate's PDS examination performance in Section A is at Master's level, examiners assess:

1. The extent to which the candidate's analysis of information illuminates the case study rather than merely summarises its content. They expect candidates to draw on their knowledge of organisational practice and research in order to give weight to their analysis and proposals.

2. The candidate's understanding of the organisation's internal context and its business environment.

3. The location of the candidate's report, paper or other in a clear business framework that gives analysis and recommendations due focus and urgency.

4. Demonstration of the candidate's ability to identify issues critical for the business, and the implications of those issues for the particular field covered by the examination questions.

5. The candidate's competence in problem-solving and in providing relevant, workable and value-adding advice or solutions.

6. The candidate's ability to present answers in ways that are appropriate, clear and well focused.

Possession of the five BACKUP competencies will enable you to achieve this kind of performance. When asked for an action plan, you may find it helpful to use a simple spreadsheet. In Chapter 4, Table 3 shows the kind of template that would have been useful in tackling the May 2004 L&D examination case study. A template like this gives an action plan impact through its visual clarity and its coverage. As you fill it in during an examination its columns will automatically remind you of the kind of information that you need to provide.

## Section B: the short questions

I am often asked whether there is a particular skill in responding to Section B questions. The answer is 'yes'. It is the skill of thinking on your feet. In everyday working life it is not difficult for any professional to be convincing in a situation – typically a meeting – where he or she knows in advance what questions to expect, where all participants are working to a formal agenda and where there has been time to do some preparation. It is far more difficult to respond effectively to unexpected questions that come in the midst of a pressured working day, or to propose relevant solutions to new problems and opportunities as and when they arise. The skill of thinking on your feet can greatly increase your professional credibility at whatever your organisational level.

Typical weaknesses that cause candidates to fail in Section B of their PDS examinations are:

- *Failure to read the question*: this results in waffle and irrelevance.

- *Failure to update professional knowledge*: this results in ignorance of important new developments, trends and debates.

- *Failure to relate an answer to a specific organisational context when asked to do so*: this makes it impossible for examiners to assess candidates' ability to relate theoretical knowledge to a practical scenario.

- *Failure, when a candidate has a ready-made example of whatever a question asks for in his or her own organisation, to evaluate his or her organisational practice instead of simply describing it*: this makes it impossible for examiners to assess how far a candidate can reflect on, and learn from, his or her organisational experience.

- *Failure to justify answers when required to do so*: many questions ask candidates to do the equivalent of 'identify and justify'. Merely responding to half of that instruction automatically loses the candidate half the available marks for that question. In practice, this means he or she cannot obtain a pass mark.

You will find further advice and sample PDS examination questions in other CIPD revision guides and core texts. A particularly useful section on how to achieve success in examinations such as these is also contained in *Employee development practice* (Stewart 1999, pp284–288). Chapter 4 of this revision guide contains examples of both weak and strong responses to various Section B L&D questions.

## Typical queries from PDS candidates

### How can I keep informed about research and wider organisational practice and apply my knowledge in a PDS exam?

Three terms are used regularly in PDS examination papers:

- *Published research*: this refers to research studies that have been published or reported in books, journals, official reports, published conference proceedings and similar.

- *Research*: this is a looser term. It can be interpreted to mean not only published research but any research, including surveys, that candidates have undertaken themselves (perhaps for their CIPD assignments or management reports, or for work projects), or that they and/or others have carried out within or outside their own organisations. When drawing on 'research' in your answers you should indicate its type and how much reliance can be placed on its findings.

- *Wider organisational practice*: information on this comes from published and more pragmatic research, from textbooks, from the Internet, from best practice and benchmarking surveys, and so on. Again, you should outline your sources when discussing such practice in an answer.

The CIPD expects PDS students to be aware of the key findings of its various research reports (each of which starts with a brief summary of conclusions or recommendations). However it does not expect specialist knowledge of them since these are expensive products that are only available from CIPD Publishing, and college and university libraries may not always stock them.

If you leave research activity until a few weeks before your examinations it will be an impossible task. Started early enough in your course of studies, it will become increasingly easy to handle. For CIPD students it involves such tasks as:

- Regularly reading the research column in the CIPD's publication *Shine*, its quarterly magazine *Impact,* and research-based articles in *People Management*.

- Regularly visiting the CIPD's research website: www.cipd.co.uk/research and using a range of Internet search engines relevant to the fields that you are studying.

- Reading textbooks and other publications that relate to the various CIPD Professional Standards and that contain up to date information about research studies and their findings. Appendix 1 provides a list of recent CIPD-sponsored research reports and similar publications that have a direct relevance for anyone working in the L&D field.

- Attending CIPD local branch talks, forums, workshops and seminars that bring participants up to date with key developments in their chosen fields and provide the opportunity for face-to-face discussion.

## What kind of textbook reading should I do?

CIPD core texts are particularly helpful – although not compulsory – reading because each is designed to cover the whole field of the Standard with which it is associated. Essentially, though, you should read any textbook whose style, content and coverage you and your tutors find best explains and illustrates the theory and practice underpinning the CIPD Standard you are studying.

**In the Section A case study where there is more than one question to be tackled, candidates are advised what amount of time**

**to spend on each. Does that indicate a particular weighting of marks attached to each question?**

No. The purpose of the advice is to make clear to candidates the kind of attention that they should give to the task associated with each question. A task that in the examiner's view should take about 70 per cent of a candidate's available time to tackle competently is clearly different from a task that should take only about 30 per cent. However, each task must be performed competently or the candidate cannot pass Section A overall.

**Do all Section B questions have equal weighting?**

Yes. Candidates can choose any seven of the 10 questions to answer. All carry the same maximum mark.

**Some Section B questions ask candidates to relate to 'your own organisation'. How can I do that if I am not currently employed, or if my organisation has no relevant examples to offer?**

On the cover of PDS examination scripts it is explained that the term 'your own organisation' can be interpreted to mean either the one where a candidate currently works or one with which they are familiar. 'Familiarity' can encompass an organisation that you know about through your own or others' experience, or one that you have read about in a textbook, on the Internet, in a journal like *People Management*, and so on. In answering such questions is important to give enough information about the organisation selected to enable the examiner to assess the relevance of your answer to that particular context. You must make clear why your proposals or observations are appropriate to 'your' organisation.

**Some Section B questions ask candidates to 'identify and justify' (or the equivalent) an answer. What are the examiners looking for here?**

I have noted earlier in this chapter that failure to 'justify' in responding to such questions automatically attracts a fail mark. This is because the examiner is requesting convincing reasons to accept the candidate's recommendations, views or statements. It is easy to propose a list of 'things to do' – most candidates can do that. It is

harder to show how the contents of that list fit the specific organisational situation outlined in a question. To do so requires the skills of
a thinking performer and a business partner. It is those skills that are
tested in such questions. You will find examples of 'identify and
justify' questions and how to tackle them in Chapter 4.

**Some Section B questions ask candidates to provide, say, 'up to
three' points about an issue. What should I do if I can only think
of one, or two?**

Where such wording is used you should try to provide three well
reasoned points. If you cannot do that, or if there is one point that for
you is vital, then you can concentrate on that without fear of penalty.
Providing that your answer is of adequate quality and is argued
convincingly it will pass.

If, on the other hand, the wording in the question is 'at least three',
then there is no option: you must produce three or your answer will
fail.

## Conclusion

The purpose of this chapter has been to provide some general information and advice about the CIPD's Professional Development
Scheme (PDS) and on how to prepare for its Master's-level Generalist
examinations. I have reflected in the chapter on some of the questions
that concern students most about the PDS examinations. This sets the
scene for a discussion of the L&D Generalist examination in Chapter 2.

# SECTION 2

## REVISION AND EXAMINATION GUIDANCE

# 2 REVISION AND EXAMINATION GUIDANCE

## Introduction

When preparing for any examination you must understand what key blocks of knowledge and practice you are expected to master. For CIPD students wishing to qualify in the L&D field, that crucial information is identified in the 'Learning and Development (L&D) Generalist Standard' and its 10 performance indicators. The purpose of this chapter is to explain the standard and the field of study that it covers.

I will first discuss the standard as a whole and then take each of its indicators in turn, focusing on some 'big issues' that make them particularly challenging and indicating types of examination questions relevant to them. From this point on you will need to keep a copy of the standard by you for regular reference. You will find a full version of it in the L&D core text *Learning and development* (Harrison 2002, pp447–450) or you can download it from www.cipd.co.uk.

## The CIPD's Learning and Development Generalist Standard

### L&D roles

L&D roles vary from smaller to larger organisations, from one organisational level to the next, and across different sectors. These variations are due to the different business environments in which L&D practitioners have to operate and to differing organisational contexts. Internal context is directly shaped by:

- vision, goals and corporate leadership related to L&D as an organisational process

- L&D's business purpose

- workplace settings, human resource (HR) practices and management's style and actions

- the type of financial and staffing base available to support L&D activity.

As explained in the core text (Chapter 8), the Institute's two-year Standards review process identified two generic roles for those with personnel and development responsibilities: those of business partner and those of thinking performer, already discussed in Chapter 1. These roles are as important in any kind of L&D work as they are in personnel work more widely.

## The L&D Generalist Standard

Like the CIPD's other professional standards, the L&D Standard is presented by reference to its:

- *Purpose:* this gives the rationale for L&D as an organisational process, and explains the type of roles likely to be held by new entrants to the field.

- *Performance indicators:* these are both operational and knowledge-based. They make clear the standard of performance in key areas of L&D activity that must be reached by those entering the field and practising in it at a basic professional level.

- *Indicative content:* This provides an outline of study topics related to each of the standard's performance indicators. Some of the indicators involve more activity areas and underpinning knowledge than others and therefore call for a wider range of topics. This does not mean that any one indicator is more important than the rest. It simply means that the knowledge base of each differs.

The standard presents L&D as an organisational process that is greater than the sum of its parts. That is why we refer to the process as 'holistic' (an organic whole) and 'integrative' (containing within that whole a number of interrelated parts). Action in one of its parts automatically changes the interaction between all of them. Each fresh L&D initiative must therefore be carefully introduced into an organisation in order to link positively with what is already in operation, as well as with wider personnel practice and business processes.

Because of their interactive nature, L&D areas of activity cannot be tackled in any neat sequence of steps. Every day L&D practitioners have to juggle with many operations at once. While trying to make a performance management system more developmental, for example, the L&D professional may also be coping with the issues arising from the management or membership of his or her small team, with designing and delivering various training and learning events, with forging business partnerships and with monitoring L&D initiatives in order to assess their added value for the business.

The aim of the L&D examination, as of all PDS examinations, is to achieve through a combination of Section A and Section B questions an adequate coverage of its Standard. I have already explained that the L&D performance indicators vary in size. There happen to be 10 of them and also 10 questions in Section B of the PDS examination, but this is accidental. It does not mean that there will be one question per indicator on every examination paper. In any one examination paper you may find (for example) two questions out of 10 in Section B that refer to different aspects of one of the biggest indicators – perhaps number 1, 2 or 7 – and no questions on one or two of the rest. Few questions will have a single focus. There are many examples of this in the examination questions contained in Chapter 4.

I will now outline each indicator of the L&D Generalist Standard and reflect on some of the big issues that each raises for students (and, often, for practitioners).

## The Standard's 10 performance indicators and some 'big issues'

### 1. Integration of L&D activity and organisational needs

Practitioners who are effective in relation to this first performance indicator co-operate with L&D stakeholders in order to integrate their activity with wider personnel and business policy and to respond to emerging challenges and opportunities. They understand and can explain convincingly to others the external environment of the organisation and its internal context.

### Big issue

This first performance indicator provides the overarching frame-work for the rest, so its scope is very wide. One 'big issue' related to it concerns the impact on national vocational education and training (NVET) policy and initiatives on organisations.

In the L&D examination I try to set questions that will enable students to relate their NVET knowledge to their own organisations. A typical question would be:

> Outline *one* national vocational education or training initiative that could be used – or is being used – in your organisation to encourage employees in their learning and development, and assess its likely benefits for your organisation

In Chapter 2 of the 2002 core text I could do no more than provide a broad-brush approach to national policy, showing the framework of vision, strategy and key challenges that acts as its context. The chapter identifies some of the biggest problems with which government has to grapple and some of the major initiatives in place in 2002, leaving it to readers to update that information. The CIPD's 2004 *Training and development survey* contains an excellent chapter (pp32–36) on the impact of government skills initiatives. There is also a useful guide on the MALPAS website. It is called the *Learning and development resource book*, and can be downloaded free from www.malpas.co.uk/downloads.

Another big issue, of course, concerns the need for L&D goals and strategy to be well aligned with the business. You can expect that all Section A case studies in L&D examination papers will be concerned in some way with the relationship between business strategy and L&D strategy (see Chapter 4 of this guide for an illustration of that in the Premier Care case, set in May 2004). Three chapters of the core text are specifically concerned with the strategic process (Chapter 3) and with the production, delivery and evaluation of L&D strategy (Chapters 4 and 5). One of the most down to earth explanations of how to create a training and development strategy is provided in *Creating a training and development strategy* (Mayo 1998). Chapter 4 in *Strategic human resource development* (Walton 1999), although going beyond PDS requirements, will give any reader a thorough appreciation of theoretical models to underpin and explain the practice of L&D strategy-making.

## 2. Provision of a value-adding L&D function

Practitioners who are effective in relation to this performance indicator are able to advise on how to achieve a well-managed, appropriately staffed and value-adding L&D function.

### Big issue

A big issue related to this second indicator concerns the need to ensure that L&D activity adds value no matter at what organisational level. This is a core task for all who hold L&D responsibilities. Failure to convince of the value-adding potential and outcomes of their activity undermines the credibility of L&D professionals.

In the May 2004 L&D examination paper I included in Section A a question that required candidates to identify some 'value-adding outcomes' for the L&D function of the organisation described in the case (see Chapter 4 of this guide). In order to respond well to such questions you need to know the theory about adding value, but you should also be able to refer to practical examples of value-adding L&D initiatives drawn from your own experience and/or from research reports or surveys (for some from the latter sources, see the core text, Chapters 4 and 5). It is also useful to have to hand some examples of failure to add value since these can make a point quite powerfully.

## 3. Contribution to the recruitment and performance management processes

Practitioners who are effective in relation to this performance indicator know how to contribute to L&D in a way that enhances the processes of recruitment and performance management (PM).

### Big issue

A big issue related to this third indicator is the need to treat PM as a process as well as a system. As a process, its purpose is to make sure that within the framework of a strategic approach to managing the business, performance targets are achieved and individual development is promoted. As a system, it has a number of interactive elements that must be skilfully managed. A typical exam question would be:

> Identify and justify some of the features that can make performance management into a powerful developmental process.

Many HR textbooks, including the core text (Harrison 2002a, p245), explain the PM process and its developmental elements. However for a good Master's-level answer to this kind of question you should not rely on theory alone. You should build into your justification some reference to research findings or to a real-life example – good or bad – that you know about. That kind of evaluative answer demonstrates real 'thinking performer' quality.

The PM process makes a vital contribution to the link between people and organisational performance, but to understand that link we need to look at other factors too. It is here that findings from the ongoing Bath University research programme headed by Professor John Purcell are so helpful (see Appendix 1). The research has confirmed the central part that training, learning and development, well integrated with other HR practices, can play in bringing the people–performance link to life.

## 4. Contribution to the retention of employees

Practitioners who are effective in relation to this performance indicator know how to contribute to career and management development strategies that will help the organisation retain and develop the people it needs for the future.

### Big issue

A big issue related to the fourth indicator is the need to build and sustain a career management system that fits the business and can change with the times. The example of SCO, a computer software company in the mid-1990s, illustrates an imaginative approach to career development in which stakeholders worked together to develop and implement the system and adapt it to ongoing needs (Harrison 2002a, p326).

Many examples of career development strategies are to be found in publications like *Career management: a guide* (King 2003). It is particularly important that you check on recent research findings on the changing psychological contract (see Appendix 1). Such information will help you to tackle examination questions like this one:

> Draw on your knowledge of published research or current trends in practice to assess how an effective career development planning process could contribute to the retention of high-calibre employees in your organisation.

## 5. Contribution to building organisational capacity and facilitating change

Practitioners who are effective in relation to this performance indicator know how to contribute to L&D in a way that will help to introduce, embed and sustain organisational change.

### Big issue

A big issue related to the fifth indicator concerns changing organisational culture. That culture is produced and continuously reinforced by workplace values and norms, organisation structure, routines and business processes, together with the myths, narratives, symbols and practices that are woven deep into the fabric of organisational life (see Harrison 2002a, pp125–128).

It is worrying to see many examination scripts where CIPD students (and indeed human resource management and development students more widely) produce naively optimistic recommendations for producing culture change. It is as if, in their minds, there is some once and for all rational prescription that can achieve that end. That prescription is usually to do with top management setting a vision, mission and strategy; communicating them; producing a plan for implementation; and then expecting the desired change to occur – all within a few months. Yet students can be forgiven, since far more experienced minds often fail to produce much greater wisdom. Prescriptions and plans are useful starting points – but no more than that. The gap between what is intended and what actually happens can be extremely wide.

The part of the PDS exam paper where you are most likely to have to demonstrate your understanding of organisational culture is in Section A. For example, in the May 2004 L&D case study (see Chapter 4 of this guide) it was important for candidates to show awareness of the need for culture change at Premier Care (the company in the case) in order to gain commitment to new vision and values, to embed recent structural changes and to prepare for more changes to come. Many missed that vital issue.

## 6. Stimulation of strategic awareness and development of knowledge

Practitioners who are effective in relation to this performance indicator know how to promote approaches to individual and collective learning that will stimulate strategic thinking, continuous improvement and innovation. These tasks are vital in the emerging knowledge-based economy.

### Big issue

One of the biggest issues related to this indicator is the need to understand the importance of the workplace as a source of organisationally valuable knowledge. It is here that the members of 'communities of practice' (those who regularly work together in shared tasks) share their tacit as well as explicit knowledge and, if they have sufficient commitment to the organisation's vision and goals, regularly apply that knowledge to continuous improvement and innovation in goods, services, products and processes. Such communities make a vital contribution to competitive capability.

Many research reports are now appearing in what is loosely called the 'knowledge management' field (some examples are shown in Appendix 1). All stress the leading role that L&D professionals should play in building and sustaining workplace environments where the creation, sharing and application of knowledge to improvement and innovation is a dominant concern. The L&D core text explains and illustrates their tasks especially in Chapters 11 and 20. A typical examination question in this area would be the following:

> Identify and explain *up to three* ways in which to develop the workplace in your organisation as a learning environment.

Alongside the theory you should become familiar with some real-life case studies that show the aids and barriers to knowledge sharing and knowledge creation in many of today's organisations (see, for example, Scarbrough and Swan 1999; Beaumont and Hunter 2002; Swart *et al* 2003; Harrison and Kessels 2003).

## 7. Design and delivery of learning processes and activity

Practitioners who are effective in relation to this performance indicator can contribute to the design and provision of effective learning processes and activity, using new technology as appropriate.

The seventh indicator is extensive in scope because it is underpinned by a wide range of concepts and theoretical models. You will find coverage in the CIPD core texts by Marchington and Wilkinson (2002) and Harrison (2002a), and in other textbooks such as Stewart (1999), Reid *et al* (2004) and Sloman (2003). Some of the most useful discussion, however, is to be found in the CIPD's research report *How do people learn?* (Reynolds *et al*, 2002), together with a related online learning module that can be downloaded from www.cipd.co.uk/howdopeoplelearn. The CIPD has also set up a Communities website in order to engage its trainer members in the shift from training to learning (www.cipd.co.uk/communities).

### *Big issue*

A big issue in relation to this major indicator is the need for collaboration between specialist L&D staff and other stakeholders in order to achieve successful learning events. In the May 2004 L&D exam paper I set the following question:

> Over coffee one of your Personnel colleagues says to you:
> "I've just read that it's out of date to base the design of learning events on the systematic training model. What do you think?"
> Provide an informed response.

You will find a discussion of that question in Chapter 4 of this guide. I mention it here because the traditional systematic training model focuses only on the functional tasks involved in planning, designing, delivering and evaluating training. However, functional skill is not enough. To achieve buy-in (external consistency) from key stakeholders, L&D practitioners also need to be skilled in *process*. That process involves operating as business partners at their organisational level.

You should reflect on the need to achieve external as well as internal consistency (these terms are explained in the L&D core text pp267–268) throughout the cycle of activity from planning to evaluation of learning initiatives and events. When preparing for the L&D examination you will find it helpful to note examples of effective and ineffective learning events, both from your own experience and from your reading. You can then relate the causes of their success or failure to the theory you have been studying. You can expand your knowledge by exchanging views and experiences with others in virtual communities similar to the one on the CIPD's training site and by accessing (for example):

- www.astd.org (the site of the American Society of Training and Development)

- http://www.trainingvillage.gr/ (the site of CEDEFOP, which is European Community funded)

- http://www.trainingzone.co.uk/ (a lively independent site)

- http://www.ukhrd.com/ (the site run by the publishers, Fenman).

## 8. Evaluation and assessment of L&D outcomes and investment

Practitioners who are effective in relation to this performance indicator know how learning outcomes can be evaluated and can advise on how to assess the likely returns on an organisation's planned future investment in L&D.

### *Big issue*

A big issue related to the eighth indicator is the need to measure the impact of L&D activity on the organisation without getting trapped in time-consuming but irrelevant measurement methods. Some outcomes can be difficult to measure – but so are some in marketing, research and development, even finance, yet they tend to attract less attention from management. Much of the pressure on L&D practitioners to 'prove it' arises not from technical problems of measurement, but from their own lack of credibility as business partners.

When preparing for the L&D examination, you should search out examples of 'good practice' L&D functions where evaluation poses few problems because of the strong business partnership between the L&D specialists and line managers – and of functions where lack of such a partnership complicates the evaluation task. The more effective the collaborative planning process, the fewer problems evaluation will usually confront.

Here is a question that I set in the May 2004 L&D examination. It could be interpreted in many ways, depending on what kind of issues candidates chose to focus on:

> If you could question your organisation's current L&D activity, what would you single out for comment, why, and what related practical proposal(s) would you make?

Here is an answer that used this question in a highly creative way, focusing especially on the importance of measuring contribution of an L&D initiative to the development of an organisation's human capital (human capital reporting is another big issue that is related to this eighth performance indicator):

> The question I would raise about my current organisation (identified by the candidate) about its current L&D activity is why it perpetuates a culture that perceives a need for development but only as a reactionary measure.
>
> In my organisation forklift drivers are needed at short notice. However when people are taken for courses that legislation requires to be five days, the operation removes them after two. Then the individual cannot be utilized and has to start again at a later date.
>
> **Proposals**
> HR to understand operational peaks and troughs, to create a human resource plan that accounts for succession planning and trains individuals during quiet periods.
>
> For HR to embrace the concept of business partner and adjust their approach to a more holistic view, collaborating with the management team to understand their problems.

To review training, learning and development as part of the monthly review incorporating a view of human capital and interpreting gained skills and knowledge as productive capital for the business.

Reviewing the L&D policy to ensure it is strategically aligned with the business strategy. The two documents must be mutually supportive as neither operates in a vacuum.

This is the answer of a true thinking performer and business partner and gained a distinction mark. I reproduce it here because, while it touches on many L&D issues, its proposals demonstrate so well the importance of well-integrated L&D initiatives and of L&D business partnerships in ensuring an effective evaluation process.

## 9. Acting as an ethical practitioner

Practitioners who are effective in relation to this performance indicator are able to identify and promote L&D processes and practices that meet or exceed legal, mandatory and ethical requirements. They understand the impact and implications of diversity of people, style, and employment contracts for L&D policies and practice and organisational learning strategies.

### Big issue

A big issue related to the ninth indicator is the complexity but profound importance of the concepts involved in ethics. L&D professionals have a responsibility to raise awareness in their organisations of ethical issues related to the learning process. They should strive to develop across those organisations the active involvement of key players in tackling those issues rather than paying little more than lip service to 'ethical behaviour'.

This, of course, takes us back to culture, the big issue examined under the fifth performance indicator. As has become apparent in a variety of contexts – certain police forces in the UK, many so-called 'caring' institutions, the top management ranks of companies like Shell and Enron – unethical behaviour can become so institutionalised that it is beyond the ability of any single professional group, let alone individual, to tackle it effectively. This strengthens the need for those entering L&D positions to have an informed understanding of basic concepts here. They should be able to identify ethical dilemmas in their own field and know how to gain support in raising awareness of the damage that, untreated, those dilemmas may cause to the business as well as to those directly involved.

In the questions that I set on ethics I try to focus on practicalities in order to make the subject come alive for candidates. Here is such a question:

> Identify *one* kind of ethical issue that can arise in a learning process or a training situation, and briefly explain why you regard it as an 'ethical' issue.

In the L&D core text, Chapter 7 explores issues of professionalism and ethics, but wider reading is advised. Chapter 13 in *Employee development practice* (Stewart 1999) is particularly good. If you want to pursue the issues in greater depth than is needed in PDS studies, you may find it useful to look at Chapter 11 of *Human resource development in a knowledge economy* (Harrison and Kessels 2003), and at Chapter 21 of *Strategic human resource development* (Walton 1999). An excellent Code of Ethics for training managers, trainers and developers has been produced in England by the Cabinet Office. It can be found on the website http://www.cmps.gov.uk or email customer.services@cmps.gsi.gov.uk

Other useful websites are:

- The Institute of Business Ethics, UK. info@ibe.org.uk, or website www.ibe.org.uk.

- Institute for Social and Ethical Accountability: website www.accountability.org.uk.

- Business for Social Responsibility – US Association: website www.bsr.org.

## 10. Ensuring continuing professional self-development

Practitioners who are effective in relation to this performance indicator are able to continuously develop their own expertise, professionalism and credibility in the L&D field.

**Big issue**

A big issue for L&D candidates in relation to this indicator is the need to take seriously their own continuing professional development (CPD) and to be well informed and innovative in their approach to it. As questions on this indicator tend to be of a more personal kind than others on an L&D paper some candidates respond to them in a very uncritical way, offering anecdotes in place of analysis and simplistic ideas instead of creative suggestions. You will find guidelines on two past questions set on this indicator in Chapter 4 (Indicator 10, questions 1 and 2). Here is another:

> Identify *three* potential barriers to the self-development process of a L&D professional, and justify how each might be tackled.

The important word here is 'justify', because you must include some evaluative content in your response to this kind of question. An answer that puts the barriers into a context – for example, by discussing the case of an L&D professional working in a small charity, or a global commercial firm – and then convinces the examiner that the approaches proposed by the candidate would work in that context will gain high marks. Such answers meet the Master's-level criteria discussed in Chapter 1.

## Conclusion

The purpose of this chapter has been to explain the L&D Generalist Standard and the field of study to which its 10 performance indicators relate, in order to help L&D students understand the criteria that govern the CIPD's L&D examination. In the following chapter I will turn to some of the most frequently asked questions by students preparing for the L&D examination, and offer advice on these.

# 3 EXAMINER'S INSIGHTS

## Introduction
............................................

The purpose of this chapter is to provide advice on preoccupations that typically concern L&D examination candidates. It has only one section. In it you will find a discussion of questions that I and members of my marking team are most frequently asked by L&D students, both on CIPD courses and on other Master's-level programmes.

## Frequently asked questions about the Learning and Development examination
.......................................................................................................................

### What is the organisational process of 'Learning and Development' and what does it offer to the business and to individuals?

There are many different definitions of L&D as an organisational process, some of them identified and explained in the L&D core text (Chapter 1). My own stresses its relationship to the development of organisationally-useful knowledge and the collaborative, ethical professional activity that it involves:

> The primary purpose of Learning and Development as an organisational process is to aid the development of knowledge and the achievement of organisational and individual goals. This involves the collaborative stimulation and facilitation of learning and developmental processes, initiatives and relationships in ways that respect and build on human diversity in the workplace.
>
> (Harrison 2002a, p7)

The L&D Standard makes clear in its 'Purpose' that L&D's most powerful outcomes for the business are to do with enhanced organisational effectiveness and sustainability, and for the individual with enhanced personal competence, adaptability and employability. L&D is a critical business process, whether in for-profit or not-for-profit organisations. As the 'Black Box' research is revealing (Purcell *et al* 2003), it is a process that is crucial in two ways:

- in equipping people with the skills they need to do their jobs

- in its potential to motivate people to apply those skills and to engage in discretionary, or 'beyond the call of duty', behaviour that can lead to above-average organisational performance.

## How can L&D generalists be effective in their organisations?

As thinking performers and business partners, L&D generalists should:

- Achieve consistency in the L&D processes and interventions that they promote or introduce. This means that they should never recommend a new L&D goal, strategy or initiative without considering how far it is likely to achieve a meaningful organisational contribution, and how well it will align with current L&D activity. L&D practitioners are there to support the business. They must show an awareness of that responsibility in all that they recommend or enact.

- Following on from that, continuously relate their operations and advice to wider HR and business policy and practice in their organisations.

- And in order to do that, create and maintain collaborative working relationships with those most involved in, and affected by, L&D activity at their organisational level.

In an article in *People Management* this year the head of people development for TNT UK emphasised the need for L&D professionals to ensure that line managers are on their side:

> It falls to us, the HR practitioners, to persuade line managers of the wisdom of training and development, the structures that need to be in place to enable us to deliver, and to highlight the rewards that will undoubtedly ensue.
>
> (James 2004)

As Chapter 6 of the L&D core text makes clear, L&D professionals must work with many partners, not least the learners themselves. Of increasing significance are union learning representatives, considered so important now that under the Employment Protection Act, 2002 they are entitled to paid time off to undertake their duties (see CIPD 2004b). There are also the official agencies that can provide L&D professionals with helpful advice and funding and give them access to networks that can support their organisational activity. Learning and Skills councils, regional development agencies, and sector skills councils are all part of what some regard as an over-complex, intrusive bureaucracy – but many L&D practitioners have forged partnerships with them that have had valuable outcomes for their organisations. Identifying some of these success stories in journals like *People Management* and applying them in appropriate ways to examination questions will always boost examination performance.

## What kind of expertise do L&D examination candidates need?

Newly qualified CIPD professionals hold a variety of roles, some quite demanding in their scope and level. L&D candidates must therefore be able to convince in their examination answers that they possess good functional knowledge coupled with a broad-based understanding of their field. They must show an ability to think and act holistically – that is to say, to take an overall 'helicopter' view of the organisation and of L&D's contribution to it – and demonstrate skill in speaking the language of the business. At their organisational level they must be informed about, and able to explain convincingly to others, the L&D implications of key challenges and opportunities that confront the business. They must be able to identify barriers to the success of L&D processes and initiatives in the workplace and how these can be tackled. They must also be able to justify the kind of support needed from other personnel practices if new L&D strategies are to be implemented effectively. All of this is the kind of know-how that is tested in the L&D examination.

In Chapter 2 I quoted a candidate's answer to a question in the May 2004 L&D exam paper to illustrate a point I was making about the eighth L&D performance indicator. I commented on the high level of that answer. Here is another, responding to the same

question in a way that demonstrates the kind of all-round quality
described in the previous paragraph:

> Currently within my organisation senior management are
> undertaking a leadership programme designed to achieve a high
> performance/coaching culture. Whilst this is useful, I would
> rather this coaching is aimed at middle managers that on the
> whole tend to have more team and people responsibilities.
>
> I would propose to introduce a development scheme for
> middle managers across the organisation to develop key skills
> in teamwork, leadership, coaching and counselling. By equip-
> ping middle management with these skills we could encourage
> a more open, honest culture where people feel empowered to
> make suggestions and become involved in project work.
>
> Currently the leadership programme is a one-off event. This
> needs to be supported by further initiatives. I would like to see
> a network of coaches/mentors established for both middle and
> senior managers to tap into the tacit knowledge throughout the
> organisation, sharing best practice and ideas on how to
> improve team effectiveness.
>
> Building such a culture would stimulate organisational
> learning and the commitment of staff. Hendry and Jenkins
> highlighted the importance of renegotiating the psychological
> contract with middle managers and these proposals, I feel,
> would begin this process in my organisation.

This answer does not indicate what kind of organisation is being
discussed or whether the proposals would have a chance of being
accepted or could be afforded, but it is so well contextualised in
other ways and is so creative and thought provoking that it gained
almost full marks.

### How can L&D students and newly qualified L&D practitioners be knowledgeable about strategy in any meaningful way when they don't operate at a strategic level?

This question reminds me of one that was posted early in 2003 in
the L&D Discussion Forum of the CIPD's flexible learning
support site. The questioner asked how to reconcile students'

need to be knowledgeable about strategy at the top level of the organisation with the fact that so many are only operating at a low organisational level and have no 'strategic' tasks to perform.

My response to this query has several parts because it raises more than one issue:

1.  It is not only students and novice practitioners who find it difficult to understand concepts like strategic thrust, vertical and horizontal integration of L&D activity, and strategic implementation. Many organisations struggle to get the balance right between formulating the 'product' of strategy, and then ensuring its effective delivery and continuous adaptation at all organisational levels. When Marks and Spencer went into freefall in the early 1990s, one reason was that the board had spent too much time dreaming up formal strategies that proved irrelevant and unfeasible to deliver (the story is in the last chapter of the L&D core text, third edition, for those interested – and of course it is still ongoing!).

2.  A hard lesson that top management of many organisations does not seem to have learned is that strategy on its own has no value. Responses to a recent CIPD survey of over 1,000 human resource/personnel professionals in senior positions in a wide variety of organisations showed that strategy documents, vision and mission statements, roadshows and team briefings to inform the workforce are only a starting point. All will go for nothing if organisational leaders, managers, and functional specialists (including L&D professionals) do not collaborate with the rest of the workforce through everyday work routines in order to build commitment, gain real involvement in implementing strategic plans, and monitor, evaluate and adapt those plans to meet new contingencies (CIPD 2003). That will ensure that 'strategising' becomes a value-adding process instead of a static product, frozen in time. The same message comes through in the Bath research findings (Purcell *et al* 2003).

3.  Many working in the L&D field are vulnerable to accusations of naivety and incompetence because they have no real idea of how the strategy process works, cannot identify or respond convincingly to big strategic issues facing the organisation (as

distinct from those issues with which they are preoccupied in their specialist silo), and do not collaborate enough with other HR colleagues in promoting value-adding initiatives for their organisations.

Essential first steps in developing knowledge and competence in the L&D strategy arena are:

- Gaining an understanding of the strategy process – how any kind of strategy is produced and of the importance here of the key players, those who sit at the strategy table influencing perceptions of information that is used to support some strategic options and to cause others to be abandoned. In the core text (Chapter 3) considerable space is devoted to a discussion of these matters, and to illustrating them in practical ways. *Creating a training and development strategy* (Mayo 1998) is of great value in clarifying the way the strategy process works in practice.

- Learning how to identify, communicate and tackle the factors that typically cause failure of many human resource (HR) strategies at implementation stage (read Hutchinson and Purcell 2003, for real insights here).

- Discovering what is involved in integrating L&D strategies and activity with other HR strategies and practice so that they get the support they need in the workplace (horizontal integration) and, beyond that, learning how both L&D and HR strategies can mesh with and inform business strategies and thereby produce added value for the business (vertical integration). All good HR and L&D texts give help here. In my own core text the most relevant single section is in Chapter 4.

In the L&D core text there is a diagram showing what a truly strategic, well-integrated L&D process looks like (Harrison 2002a, p11). Here, it is helpful to look at an answer one candidate gave to a question in an L&D exam. about strategy. The question asked for an example of 'integrative' L&D activity and an explanation of how it was integrative. This is what the candidate wrote:

> It is vital that Learning and Development practitioners are integrated vertically with the strategic aims and business objectives

of their organisation and horizontally with wider HR and operational practices. A key method for the L&D practitioner to be
'integrative' is in establishing strong links with line managers.
As a great deal of learning and development responsibility is
being devolved to line managers it is vital that the L&D practitioner is aware of operational issues and constraints and how
L&D must match the reality of the organisational context if it is
to be effective in adding value to the organisation.

The answer is simple yet shows an understanding of strategy in an
L&D context. It confuses the issue by referring to practitioners being
integrated, instead of to integration of the activities in which they
are involved. But it does explain in adequate outline what is meant
by horizontal and vertical integration, and it does suggest how to
achieve horizontal integration at one level – that of the business unit.
The example is not related to any particular organisational scenario
but it provides enough practical information and insight for a pass
mark. Strategy does not have to be a complex thing – indeed if it is,
you can be sure it will not work!

## How can L&D examination candidates demonstrate 'strategic ability' and the related qualities of a thinking performer?

Candidates can do this by showing an understanding of the strategy
process, by being able to identify the difference between what has been
intended and what is really going on in an organisation, and by producing feasible practical recommendations to implement corporate or
business unit strategies at their own organisational level.

The place that offers most scope to demonstrate this understanding and competence is in Section A of the PDS examination paper. In
responding to the case study questions you need an understanding
of how strategy (of whatever kind and whether at corporate, unit or
functional level) is developed and produced, and of the forces that
influence its production. You must also show awareness of how
strategy should be implemented and continuously adapted through
everyday operations in the workplace.

Usually you will be able to demonstrate that awareness in your
practical proposals and/or action plan. You should make clear how
your proposals or plan can be communicated and implemented in

ways that will ensure relevance, feasibility and will be likely to gain widespread commitment. You should identify and explain how to tackle any barriers to acceptance or implementation, and you should make clear who should be accountable for putting the various elements of your plan into action. More suggestions about tackling case study questions are given in Chapters 1 and 4.

## How is the performance of candidates assessed in the L&D examination?

The L&D Standard provides 10 indicators to aid assessment of candidates' performance. Each performance indicator has its operational aspects and a related knowledge base. The L&D examination primarily tests candidates on the Standard's knowledge indicators, since its operational indicators are the focus of assignments and management reports. However, there can be no absolute distinction between operational competence and knowledge, so the L&D examination seeks also to generate evidence of candidates' grasp of the more intellectual elements of the operational indicators such as analytical and diagnostic ability and action-planning competence.

In Chapter 4 you will find examples of the kinds of answers to examination questions that typically gain high marks, and of those that tend to attract only a bare pass mark or a fail.

## How can I perform well in the examination if I do not work in an L&D function or have any exposure to it?

This is a very frequently asked question. Basic advice includes:

- Try to get involved in projects at work that have an L&D aspect to them.

- Form relationships with L&D colleagues whether in the your own organisation or some other and use them to expand L&D knowledge and understanding (co-students are particularly helpful here).

- Find a mentor who has special L&D expertise and can  also introduce you to various L&D networks.

- Get as much information about L&D at the practical level as possible through observing L&D activity in your own organisation and through visiting various training websites, including the CIPD's, online training communities and so on.

**The L&D field seems vast and its boundaries very fluid. How can I best prepare for the examination?**

Everyone has his or her own best way of preparing for an exam. There are many information sources, not least your tutors, to give you guidance on time management, mind-mapping and other tools helpful to your revision and examination process. I will not attempt to detail these here.

Apart from the suggestions in Chapter 4, the best advice I can give you is to aim for full familiarity with the L&D Standard discussed in Chapter 2. It is surprising how many candidates seem ignorant of its content. The standard lays out the L&D field, explains its purpose and provides the indicators against which you will be assessed. Its indicative content suggests key study topics.

You should regularly test your understanding of the standard by relating your reading and coursework to it, by tackling past examination questions and checking your answers against examiner's reports (for CIPD national examinations these can be downloaded from the CIPD's website, www.cipd.co.uk), by organising your course notes around its indicators, and by continually updating your reading and research knowledge through accessing journals such as *People Management* and relevant books, reports and websites (see Appendix 1). All of this activity will form a discipline that, if you develop it from the early stages of your course of study, will gradually become habitual. By the time you reach your immediate pre-examination period it should then be relatively straightforward to cover the essential ground in your revision.

Remember, too, that everything you learn as you tackle assignments and management reports will have a use in your examination preparation too. Few candidates seem to bring the knowledge that they have acquired from these activities into the examination room, yet it can be invaluable in informing responses to examination questions.

**What happens if, during the examination, I run out of time in an answer but I have made some relevant rough notes in the 10-minute exam reading time?**

No marks can be given for rough notes as they stand, in this or any other CIPD examination. However, if you refer explicitly in your answer to a particular point or set of points you have made in rough, and if your rough notes are attached to your script (as they should be in any case), the L&D markers will take those points into account when marking your examination answer. Of course this does not mean that you should rely on rough notes. All it means is that, in a situation where you have clearly run out of time, the markers will be sympathetic to all your attempts to indicate relevant thinking.

Practice in time management throughout your course of study, and again in your revision, should considerably reduce the likelihood that you will run out of time in the examination. But panic does play a part here. One final tip, therefore, is never to look back. Once you have started to answer your chosen examination questions, do not let yourself be distracted by the thought that your last answer didn't feel as if it was a good one. You may score nothing for one of your seven Section B answers and do indifferently on a few more, but you can still make up enough lost ground to pass if you do well with the rest. Looking back – as mountaineers know – can cause a fatal fall. So try to put that previous answer out of your mind and press ahead with the next question, refusing to let one small possible failure destroy your confidence. If you have prepared well and have a sound theoretical and practical understanding of the standard and its indicators, your chance of gaining a pass grade will always be high.

## Conclusion

The purpose of this chapter has been to provide advice on preoccupations that typically concern L&D examination candidates. Some are about Learning and Development as a field of study. More questions of that type, with feedback on them, are contained in Chapter 1 of the L&D core text.

Nothing is as helpful to students, however, as the opportunity to look at ways in which questions typical of those they can expect are and can be answered. This information is provided in the following chapter, which, because I appreciate its importance for you, is by far the longest in this revision guide.

# SECTION 3

**EXAMINATION PRACTICE AND FEEDBACK**

# 4 EXAMINATION QUESTIONS AND FEEDBACK

## Introduction

This chapter has three aims:

- to suggest ways of reaching Master's-level standard in the L&D Generalist examination

- to provide a selection of questions typifying those that can be expected in L&D examinations that follow the PDS format and that are pitched at Master's level

- to illustrate how such questions can be tackled and in so doing to help readers expand their understanding of the L&D Standard's 10 performance indicators on which the questions are focused.

The chapter starts with some general advice for L&D candidates. It then looks at Section A questions set for the CIPD's Learning and Development examination in May 2004 and provides feedback on those.

That section is followed by one that provides 20 Section B L&D questions that have appeared since the first PDS diet in May 2003. The questions are shown under the L&D performance indicators to which they primarily relate. However, because the indicators relate to areas that in real life dynamically interact, it is rarely the case that any question is solely concerned with one indicator. Most cover aspects of others also.

The feedback on Section A and Section B questions incorporates examples of answers produced by past L&D candidates together with comments on those.

## Reaching Master's-level standard

In Chapter 1 I explained why the PDS qualification is officially recognised as being at Master's level, and the concepts of 'thinking performer' and 'business partner' and the BACKUP framework that underpin the PDS Standards and examinations.

In the L&D examination you can achieve Master's-level standard in the following ways:

- *By dealing with complex issues systematically and creatively.* You must get to the heart of the matter, whether in the case study or in a Section B question. You must make sense of the case scenario, separating what counts from what, essentially, does not. You must produce recommendations or plans that are logical given that scenario.

- *By making sound judgements in the absence of complete data.* In an examination paper, as in your daily work, you will never be presented with all the information you need. So you must make do with what you have. Drawing on careful analysis of that information and on your experience, knowledge of research and of wider organisational practice you must convince that your judgements are well informed and can be relied on.

- *By achieving originality in tackling and solving problems.* Remember that relying on popular theories and well established 'best practice' to help drive an organisation forward has two drawbacks: such theories and practice are well-known and so can be copied by other organisations; and they are not tailored to any specific organisation's needs and context. Originality is about knowing how to adapt the general to the particular and make of it something unique. Organisations that produce unique knowledge, products, processes and services are the ones that forge ahead.

- *By planning and advising on how to implement tasks at your professional level*: for the purposes of any PDS examination that is taken to be the basic business unit level.

- *By proposing/making convincing, feasible and ethical decisions in complex and unpredictable situations*: convincing to your audience, whether in the organisational or examination context; feasible given the factors that are likely to help or hinder the implementation of those decisions; and ethical by your own professional and personal standards. Ethics is a minefield. However, you will find later in this chapter that some PDS candidates are already showing real promise in their ability to identify ethical issues for L&D practitioners and in their ideas about how to respond to ethical dilemmas in the L&D field.

- *By communicating your conclusions clearly to various types of audience.* Our HR profession is one of the most frequently criticised for its use of jargon, 'touchy-feely' language and obscure terminology. An article in one of the quality newspapers leapt out at me the other day for the enraged attack that its author made on HR practitioners who use terms like 'business partners', 'bottom line', 'human capital reporting', 'human resource management', 'downsizing' and 'a learning culture'. We take such terms for granted, but they inflame many outside the HR profession. When writing a response to a Section A or a Section B question you should therefore use a style, a structure and a language that communicates your message to your audience clearly and in relevant language.

As you read the examination questions in this chapter, note how they call for demonstration of thinking performer, business partner and BACKUP qualities, and look for the presence of the six features that I have just described in the sample answers you will find here.

## L&D Generalist examination questions and feedback: Section A

### Case study, May 2004

The private sector Premier Care Group provides and manages residential housing and community care support for the elderly and for people with learning disabilities. It was reorganised last year and further restructuring is likely in the next two or three years as the Group continues to expand.

There are currently 500 employees working in a flattened structure with three divisions:

- The division containing head office functions. Head Office is based in a major city, and housing is located across surrounding counties.

- The Care division, which employs care workers. They are based in about 40 houses located throughout the Group's territory. Each house has a manager and a team of care workers looking after up to five residents. The care workers work in shifts.

- The Housing division, which employs housing officers (who deal with tenants' housing problems) and trades people (who carry out property repairs). The trades people work from home and travel about their areas in company vans. Since reorganisation they have been connected to their managers by laptops, emails and so on – indeed every employee at Premier Care now has a computer or easy access to one, and a company intranet is being developed.

Currently, there are two internal problems that need a speedy resolution:

- Premier Care is well known for its strong dedication to its clients and most of its staff are long-serving and highly committed. But the Group is not unified. It lacks a sense of common values and purpose, and communications between its divisions are poor.

- After reorganisation management responsibility was devolved, with care managers and housing managers being given budgetary control and responsibility for staffing and training in their divisions. As yet, however, many lack the skills needed to carry out their new responsibilities.

The Group's small personnel and development (P&D) function is located at headquarters. The P&D Manager reports to the company secretary and manages three qualified P&D staff together with a secretary and an office junior. In addition to helping the Group tackle the above problems, the function has a couple of other challenges to meet:

- The Group invests a lot in staff training, achieved Investors in People (IiP) status in 2000 and is coming up to its second IiP review in six months' time. However, there has never been any evaluation of the organisational impact of the learning and development (L&D) investment. From now on the P&D Manager must report annually to the Board on that impact.

- By 2006 the Group must achieve the government target of 50 per cent of care staff having a minimum of NVQ level 2 and 50 per cent of managers having NVQ level 4. At present only about a quarter of these personnel have the required qualifications.

The P&D Manager is meeting the company secretary shortly in order to agree a Learning and Development (L&D) plan for Premier Care in the coming year. As one of the three P&D generalists, you have been given the task of producing a discussion paper for her to aid this meeting. In it, you must:

1.  Identify and justify the main value-adding outcomes for L&D activity to achieve in the coming twelve months. You should draw on wider organisational practice and on published research findings as well as on an analysis of case study data to give your arguments conviction

2.  Draft a feasible, well-explained plan to achieve those outcomes.

Please produce this paper.
(You should spend about 40 per cent of your time on task 1, and about 60 per cent of your time on task 2.)

## Feedback and advice on the case study

My examiner's report on the May 2004 L&D examination covers the case study in detail. It can be downloaded from the CIPD's website (www.cipd.co.uk). The following additional comments incorporate examples of candidates' answers.

### Question 1

In responding to this question candidates needed to look both at L&D implications of the broad-based organisational issues high-lighted in the bullet points on the first page of the study, and at the more specific L&D issues highlighted later. Candidates had to decide which issues to prioritise in order to produce the most value-adding L&D outcomes in the coming twelve-month period.

Here is one answer to the first question:

> *Main value-adding outcomes*
> 1. First we have to address – communications plan/strategy. Based on Kotter's model for organisational change,

Premier Care Group need a 'communication strategy' in order to address the current problem with poor communication between decisions. The Company Secretary needs to communicate his mission/vision/values – key stakeholders need to be consulted – 'participative policy making' (one of Pedler et al) Learning Organisational disciplines – representatives from each division. Communications was a vital element during the John Lewis change of opening hours in order to win the hearts and minds of staff. Staff need to know company's vision in order to understand their objectives etc.

2. Managers need to be trained in budgetary control/HR and training (to include evaluation in order to address the IIP issue) Management Development Programme.

3. Resources to be offered to staff/managers in order to reach their NVQ targets.

4. Career Development for staff to maintain commitment.

This kind of answer does not gain a pass. It does focus on the specifics of the question by trying to identify some value-adding outcomes, but apart from the first point there is no attempt to provide justification for the candidate's choice. There is no explanation of the purpose of the paper, no identification of who its author is meant to be or of the person to whom it is addressed, and no reference to Premier Care's business environment or internal context. (You may think that in a draft paper these omissions do not matter, but they do because they provide a clear framework for that paper. Even just a two or three sentence outline would show your awareness of the need for that.) The four 'outcomes' represent random surface issues only. There are two references to research/wider organisational practice and with more explanation these might have been helpful. However because neither has been related clearly to the Premier Care scenario they do not add to our understanding of the case.

Contrast the following answer:

*Introduction*
Premier Care is a well-established organisation with a committed and long serving pool of employees. Currently we are

undergoing substantial change and there is a need to ensure all our staff are informed and committed to the future of Premier Care.

Along with this we currently have a skills gap within our management population and we must seek to rectify this.

*L&D Activity for the Future*

Learning and development should exist to enhance organisational capability, cost effectively building the skills and knowledge Premier Care needs to gain competitive advantage.

To add value to the organisation through this challenging period L&D must integrate with:

organisational vision and strategy

HR policy and practice

the current employment system

In order to do this, we must undertake the role of change agent as researched by Dave Ulrich. To this end I see four main value-adding outcomes for the function to achieve over the next twelve months:

*1. Development of shared vision and values*

Staff competence, flexibility and commitment are the key to organisational success. Guest et al found in their research that this is generated through linking business strategy, HR strategy and HR practices. We must therefore provide a mechanism to generate a mutuality of interest amongst our key stakeholders and define our organisational vision.

*2. Management development*

Local managers within flatter organisational structures are the key to organisational success and we must make it a priority to ensure that our managers are equipped with the skills to drive the organisation forward. In a government paper 21st Century Skills: Realising our Potential, the skills gap was (indecipherable) with 39 per cent of employees having low skills and few – 28 per cent – being educated to intermediate level. There is a need therefore to introduce learning to develop higher NVQ skills at levels 4 and 5.

*3. Evaluation of learning*

In order to justify the cost of our learning interventions and to prepare us for IIP reassessment we must formalise evaluation of our organisational learning. We must pass reassessment and must be able to justify our training expenses. CIPD research shows that only 50 per cent of those who took part in the Who Learns at Work survey were asked about the impact of the learning they undertook. We must rectify this or how can we show it adds value, but the Kirkpatrick model of Evaluation has been deemed inappropriate by many authors/academics including Harrison and the Training Organisation.

*4. Continuing Professional Development*

By introducing a culture of continuous learning and recognising individuals' success we can improve the knowledge and skills base within the organisation enabling us to respond effectively and quickly to the continuing changes in our environment. With a fairly static workforce we need to look for other ways of acquiring this knowledge.

This second answer is a distinction-level response to the first question, demonstrating all the qualities emphasised at the start of this chapter. It hits big organisational issues (although missing the need for an increased acquisition of level 2 NVQs as well as the higher levels). It identifies a small cluster of value-adding L&D outcomes to be achieved (and the candidate went on in the plan to take each of these in turn, explaining how to translate them into action). It draws explicitly on research (although getting one reference wrong – I am not aware that I ever unreservedly condemned Kirkpatrick!). Knowledge of good practice is implicit in the way that the candidate has analysed the data, in the insights drawn from it, and in the proposals made. Finally it is well presented: it is clearly structured, concise, focuses throughout on the specifics of the question and uses straightforward business language.

### Question 2

Here, candidates had to provide plans that tied in with the issues identified in response to Question 1 and show how their proposals could be translated into action. To convince that it was 'feasible and well-explained' any plan should have included some information on allocation of responsibilities for its elements, on timing, and on resources needed. It should have demonstrated business partnership process and paid attention to any links needed to other business and HR policies

Here is an example of a pass-level answer to this question:

### *Learning and Development Plan*
*Introduction*

The P&D will add value to Premier Care Group by encouraging individuals to learn and by enabling the organisation to share in its knowledge and skills to develop to its full potential.

*P&D Plan*

**Objective 1**

The P&D team has three qualified officers led by the P&D manager. During the first quarter of this year the team are implementing an evaluation procedure. This is being led by our qualified Internal Reviewer who will design and construct the paperwork and reporting results which will be available on the intranet. Each course application will require objectives and an evaluation and assessment which will be followed up at quarterly points by the team if not completed.

**Objective 2**

The P&D team will set up a local NVQ contract with the local college to enable a qualified assessor and internal verifier to help our staff achieve the NVQ Standards required. During this year we aim to start 20 per cent of our care staff and 10 per cent of our managers on an NVQ, which should be completed within 12 months. Their progress is recorded by the College and fed into the P&D team who will monitor this scheme.

**Objective 3**

The P&D will be setting up a working group to look at unifying the group's goals and direction. Each member of staff will be contacted by email to request for volunteers to join this group. The email will include the opportunities available to those on the working group as to what is expected from them. The group will be facilitated by the P&D manager who will then put the group's ideas forward to the company secretary for approval before being publicised.

**Objective 4**

The P&D manager and one of his team will be scoping training providers to deliver a CD-Rom and intranet based computer based training package. This will be provided to all managers by quarter 2 who will be required to complete by the end of quarter 4. The manager will be supported in local discussion groups which will be facilitated by one of the P&D team. Managers will gain skills in budgeting, appraisal, feedback and training needs analysis.

*Summary*

This is a draft plan that I believe will enable the group to make its first step forward to providing a value-adding service. It is important that we record the results of our activity and the outcomes achieved to enable us and the company to see the benefits of the P&D team and our contribution.

During the meeting you may like to point out the benefits which other organisations have benefited on by using similar ideas and processes. This can include the Royal Bank of Scotland who during takeover of the NatWest were able to provide quality e-learning packages to their staff who then demonstrated a higher learning standard due to this method of training.

A number of other organisations such as Marks and Spencer have set up working groups to help managers decide the future success of their company. The working group can act as a good sounding board for management and staff alike.

Please let me know if there is any more information that you require. I would be interested in any feedback on my plan and from your meeting with the Company Secretary.

This plan is competent enough for a clear pass. It covers some important issues, has some useful practical detail and makes an attempt at a timescale. It includes persuasive references to wider organisational practice (the candidate in answering Question 1 had already referred, although minimally, to relevant research in the form of the CIPD's T&D 2004 survey that related to the value of bite-sized training). It is clearly presented and uses appropriate language given that it is a discussion paper for the author's manager.

However, the plan has no clear strategic framework either at business or L&D level – its introductory sentence is far too vague for that. It is quite narrowly focused and its elements are primarily operational. It makes no links to crucial HR or business processes such as performance management, relations and rewards. It is short on business partnerships within the organisation, failing to indicate (other than in Objective 3 and in a brief and passing comment in Objective 4) how it might gain the active commitment of managers to the actions it proposes. While making a number of suggestions that will be costly in terms of expertise, time and money, it does not identify even a generalised resource base. There is an attempt to link its four objectives to issues discussed in the candidate's answer to Question 1 (not reproduced here), but that link is not always clear enough. Indeed one important element of that answer – the need for a 'management development programme' that goes beyond the skills that Premier Care's managers currently lack – is not discussed in the plan. Some major issues at Premier Care are also ignored, notably the need to prepare for the forthcoming IiP review, and to develop a workforce that can adapt to the new organisation structure and also be flexible in the face of future changes. The whole answer only skims the surface of the crucial issue of culture change.

A different type of answer (or part of it) is shown in Table 3. The candidate used this template to generate information that convinced that the plan was 'feasible and well explained'. The extract shown in the table incorporates thoughtful, strategically focused detail that responds fully to the requirements of Question 2. This answer was at distinction level.

## L&D Generalist examination questions and feedback: Section B

In this section you will find two questions for each of the L&D Standard's 10 performance indicators, together with feedback on these. For ease of reading I have taken each indicator, its associated questions and feedback on them, in turn. Where a question raises a variety of issues or deals with matters that many students may find new and puzzling, the feedback given is proportionally longer than for questions that deal with more familiar or less complex topics.

I have made no attempt to suggest model answers. It would be misleading to do so. In the L&D field there are no 'one best way' prescriptions. L&D professionals must respond to each new challenge as thinking performers and business partners. They must use relevant theory, experience, and knowledge of wider organisational practice

**Table 3** An action planning template: extract from a candidate's answer to Section A, Question 2, May 2004 L&D Case Study.

| L&D Activity | How to provide | Who will provide | Cost | Benefit | Timing; any wider HR implications |
|---|---|---|---|---|---|
| 1. L&D strategy. | Work with the Co. Secretary to review business goals & objectives and then work with P&D group to align P&D strategy & integrate L&D strategy & activity accordingly. | P&D Manager; P&D generalists who work on P&D policies, practices & procedures. | Internal time of Co. Secretary, P&D manager & P&D generalists. | L&D strategy, policies & procedures given direction, vision, values to frame delivery of L&D in workplace. | Month 1. Identify any problems in integrating P&D or L&D strategies & practices. |
| 3. Workplace learning including coaching, mentoring & NVQs. | Train managers as trainers and as coaches, providing feedback & devel. teams. Use external NVQ assessors initially. Aim longer-term to develop and train our own NVQ assessors. | Managers; P&D staff; external consultants. | Training managers will be costly, but will probably need to use external expertise as we do not have enough of our own at present. Say 60 managers trained over 3 days Each @ £1k per day, £180K + indirect costs. | Managers trained & can train staff, so though high up-front costs, should get pay-back & then added value after first year. | Management training from months 2 – 7. Assessor training could start towards year end or move into early 2nd year with new budget + some external funding as an NVQ & IIP-related initiative. |

**Table 3 continued**

| L&D Activity | How to provide | Who will provide | Cost | Benefit | Timing; any wider HR implications |
|---|---|---|---|---|---|
| | | | Further costs to use external assessors, & later train our own. Seek help of LSC to advise here. | | Has implications for performance mgmt. process and for reward policy & job evaluation. |
| 4. Online learning & coaching. | Buy system & adapt to Premier's needs & L&D strategy. | P&D; IT Mgr./ external consultant. | £8K – £12K | Online learning for all types of staff, including home workers. | Pilot in months 3 – 7 then establish. Appraisal system? Reward policy? |

and of research findings to work out possible solutions. Any chosen solution must fit organisational context, add value where it matters most and be able to be implemented satisfactorily in the workplace.

Full coverage of the Section B questions that appeared in the May 2004 examination paper is contained in my examiner's report that can be downloaded from the CIPD's website. I have not reproduced that feedback here. Instead I have given space to examples of candidates' answers and discussion of those.

## Indicator 1: integration of L&D activity and organisational needs

### Question 1
*Identify one major national training or vocational educational initiative introduced during or after 2001 and assess some key practical implications for employers. (November 2003)*

This question relates to topics covered in the second part of Indicative Content 1.1. Chosen initiatives had to be post-2000, since an important aim in this question was to test how far candidates' knowledge of national VET initiatives was up to date.

Here is one type of answer that came up fairly regularly in the scripts:

> One major national training/vocational educational initiative that has recently been introduced is 'Lifelong Learning'. Following pressure from employee unions the Labour government now considers it is one of the many 'planks' of government policy and it is designed to stimulate and support adult learning throughout the working life.
>
> In today's volatile economic climate prolonged periods of employment in one company is unlikely for the vast majority therefore lifelong learning is aimed at providing access for people to acquire and develop new skills and knowledge to present them with greater employment opportunities.
>
> The concept of the initiative permits people to learn about both work and non-related topics/skills often in their own time.
>
> The implications for employers are:
> • To use lifelong learning to complement work-related training

- To help provide physical facilities for learning
- To support the appointment of lifelong learning reps from within the workplace thus accepting the loss of time of those elected
- As learning increases employees expectations increase; consider retention strategies
- Morally the company may wish to extend the process financially to include family participation.

Despite its length, this kind of answer is unlikely to be awarded many marks. It does not answer the question, being about a generalised policy not a specific initiative and also referring to a policy introduced long before 2001. It is also confused in its focus and in the practical points it makes.

Here, by contrast, is an answer that gained a distinction:

*Union Learning Reps*
In the 2001 White Paper the government introduced Union Learning Reps to aid their commitment to lifelong learning, and in their 2003 White Paper they confirmed their continued support for this initiative.

At (a named organisation) we have a recognised trade union (named) with shop stewards in place to represent the workforce. However, neither the union nor the company have introduced this new initiative of union learning reps at this moment.

The practical implications that the company would need to consider would be:

- How will the Union Learning Reps (ULRs) work in line with business strategy and goals?
- What responsibilities will the reps have and how will this fit in with the overall L&D plans?
- How will the ULRs work in the operation and will they provide learning and development opportunities and promote the initiatives that the training and  development team already have?
- Will they provide the same for union and non-union members?

In order to introduce such an initiative would mean working in partnership with the union, the business and the training and development function to establish how they could add value and achieve a positive result for everyone.

Despite a small error at the start, such answers score highly. They focus completely on the question; they make use of a real-life case, all the more striking in this example because it is a negative one, to illuminate the implications of their chosen initiative; they demonstrate up-to-date knowledge of that initiative and its place in national policy; they show the qualities of a thinking performer in their strategic emphasis, their integrative approach (shown especially in the first three of the four bullet points) and their reflective stance; and they make clear the need for a unique set of business partnerships in any organisation intending to introduce this kind of initiative.

## Question 2
*Drawing on your knowledge of wider organisational practice/ published research, identify up to three of the most significant challenges facing L&D as an organisational process and explain why you think they are so important. (May 2003)*

This question asks for up to three challenges and ideally three should be given. However, if you only gave one, or two, a pass would still be awarded if the 'challenge' was convincing and well argued.

The wording of the question allowed candidates to focus on any significant challenges in the external or internal environment of organisations. However, to gain a pass they had to draw on knowledge of published research or of organisational practice that went wider than their own organisations. Obvious sources of information are the L&D core text (for an outline of current challenges and practice, see Chapter 1, pp20–26); the CIPD's annual Training and Development survey and summaries of findings from the Institute's stream of research reports (see Appendix 1); and the CIPD report, *Training in the knowledge economy* (Stewart and Tansley 2002).

Here is an answer that gained high marks:

> There are a number of challenges facing the L&D function including:
> - The devolvement of L&D to line managers, due to an increasing belief in HR as a shared responsibility. In some

organisations this has reduced the need for a specialised L&D department. However it is vital that the learning practitioner remains, in order to ensure that learning initiatives are not set aside under the pressure of operational demands and that their effectiveness in adding value is monitored and evaluated.

- Due to international competition and recession a number of organisations have been forced to reduce costs through downsizing. L&D practitioners are threatened by this downsizing, as organisations are not always able to invest in training due to financial difficulty. However it is important that L&D function remains in some strategic form even if its day-to-day operations are reduced or outsourced. This is in order to ensure the alignment of L&D objectives and activity with the long-term strategic aims of the company.
- Another challenge facing L&D as an organisational process is the emergence of e-learning. As many companies are keen to introduce cost effective and efficient e-learning packages the role of the training manager is often reduced. However L&D practitioners can overcome this challenge by moving away from the traditional roles of training manager/passive provider to one of strategic facilitator/ internal consultant.

This kind of answer identifies three challenges and convinces that they are significant. It considers in each case how the L&D practitioner can respond proactively. Without naming any specific source of reference it demonstrates knowledge of current trends in organisational practice in the L&D field identified in recent CIPD Training and Development surveys, as well as of some relevant research findings.

### Indicator 2: provision of a value-adding L&D function

#### Question 1
*You are going to talk to the CIPD's local branch about how the L&D function can add value for the business. The Chair has told you that your audience 'wants practical insights, not dry as dust theory'. Outline and justify some key points you will make in your talk. (May 2003)*

This question focuses on the eighth as well as the second performance indicators since it involves making a business case for L&D activity. A good answer could incorporate references to one or more L&D initiatives known to the speaker that have been successful in adding value and in helping individuals, teams or the collective organisation to better achieve business goals. Obvious examples would be initiatives that have:

- resulted in cost reduction

- resulted in income generation

- helped to protect the organisation and its employees – for example through effective equal opportunities or health and safety training programmes

- eased the path of culture change, of the introduction of new technology, or of any other organisational change.

The wording of such a question makes it clear that candidates cannot pass by simply providing a list of points. They must also produce a persuasive rationale. They should take into account here that the audience for the talk will be people from a local CIPD branch, who will therefore be well informed about personnel and development matters.

### Question 2
*You are a training consultant planning a course to train inexperienced L&D staff from various organisations to become 'business partners' at their level. Draw on good organisational practice to outline and justify the main topics that you will cover in your course. (November 2003)*

This question refers especially to the areas covered by Indicative Content 2.7 of the second performance indicator, relating to business partnerships. At a secondary level it could also be interpreted as relating to the seventh performance indicator, in that it touches on content of a learning event.

Here is one type of answer that cropped up quite often:

Main topics which I would cover for a course dedicated to becoming a Business Partner would be:

- Ensure L&D strategy is in line with organisational goals and objectives in order to ensure synergy.
- Liaise and communicate effectively with the board advising on current issues.
- Ensure you are aware of business activity. Keep 'your finger on the pulse', ensuring full knowledge of daily occurrences to prevent any surprises.
- Assess organisational L&D strategy and analyse, considering any improvements and only recommending if cost effective and timely.
- Undertake a Job Training Analysis in order to identify any areas in need of vital learning and development – utilising a suitable approach dependent on time available, maybe a comprehensive analysis if time allows or problem centred analysis to identify root causes or issues if necessary.

Such an answer lists a number of points but does not justify any. It is therefore impossible to be clear about their relevance to the specifics of the question. Some of the points made in the answer represent actions that would in fact be carried out by effective business partners, but equally they could refer to actions taken simply by business-focused L&D practitioners – of itself, not necessarily the same thing. Also there are many topics that would be essential to include in such a course that receive no mention here. Overall, a fail mark, possibly in the marginal fail category, is all that can be awarded to this kind of answer.

Here is a very different response:

In order to operate competently as a business partner it is essential that L&D staff can work towards the strategy of the organisation, adding value in the development and continuous improvement of staff, and by understanding what the business aims are so it can anticipate how staff need to develop in the future to meet those aims. It is essential therefore that the L&D staff ensure that they are:

- Horizontally integrated: i.e. their L&D policies link into all other HR processes in the organisation.
- Vertically integrated: i.e. their L&D policies are aligned with the corporate strategy and departmental strategies.

It is also essential to understand the organisation's structure, hierarchy and politics in order to understand how L&D will be positioned in the organisation.

And you need to be aware of all the partnerships you'll need to work with:

- Directors
- Managers
- Staff
- L&D/HR teams
- As well as shareholders and external parties (LSCs, educational institutions, etc) who may influence funding.

It is also critical to understand the business context, strategy, competitors etc. in order to be seen to be credible. You will need to 'market' or 'sell' your services to the business and demonstrate how you can assist in the achievement of its objectives.

This kind of answer is worth at least a merit mark. It does not explicitly refer to topics or to 'inexperienced' L&D staff, but it is clear that its content would be relevant for the kind of course envisaged in the question. The candidate never spells out what is meant by a 'business partner', but the skills and knowledge indicated do make clear enough some key ways in which L&D staff will need to work with others in order to achieve their goals. There is no explicit reference to good practice, but the content shows a fair grasp of relevant theory and practice.

### Indicator 3: contribution to the recruitment and performance management processes

#### Question 1
*Your Personnel Director says to you, the organisation's L&D manager, "What I need from your function this year is a strong contribution to this company's performance management process. What do you suggest?" Outline a convincing reply. (May 2003)*

There are many ways of answering this kind of question:

- One way is to focus on the concept of performance management as a cycle incorporating the L&D processes of induction, job-related training, appraisal and personal development. Such an answer could propose an integrative approach to those processes, or could target the improvement of one of them in order to ensure a more effective performance management process overall.

- Another is to focus on the difficulty of balancing control and development in many performance management systems, and propose ways of improving the balance while ensuring that there is a strong link between the individual's objectives and those of their department and of the organisation as a whole.

- Another way is to suggest that a strong contribution from the L&D function can only achieve results if there is a business partnership between L&D staff, HR staff and line managers – and propose ways of achieving that. Since we know from research (see Hutchinson and Purcell 2003) that any process fundamental to the linking of people to organisational performance requires the active and informed involvement of front-line management if it is to work, a proposal to provide advice and training for such managers would be particularly effective here.

PM systems often fail because they are too complicated to implement effectively, so any candidate pointing out the need to keep the system simple if it is to make an impact would gain marks for that. There is also a need to be a thinking performer when confronted with this kind of scenario and question what if any value the system is adding, and how relevant and clear are its aims.

### Question 2
*A high street bank has just devolved most of its Human Resource (HR) responsibilities to its line managers. Produce a reasoned reply to the following email sent to you, the L&D manager located at headquarters, by the HR Director:*
*'A priority task for our managers is to recruit some new key workers, but most of them haven't the skills to do that competently. What should we do about this?' (May 2004)*

Compare the following two responses to this question:

*Answer 1*

Following devolution of some HR activities, I understand that line managers will be undertaking some recruitment for key workers. They will need to develop their skills in order to do this. I would recommend them undertaking our internal recruitment and selection course which covers such topics as relevant legislation, discrimination issues, pitfalls such as halo/horns and stereotyping and following the process through to induction.

The company has recently introduced a competency framework and therefore any interviews should be competency-based. The managers may therefore need some self-development in these competencies to allow improved business understanding. They will need support in the process, either from yourselves in HR of from us, and we are happy to undertake it. Perhaps someone sitting in for their first few interviews will increase their confidence.

I would also suggest having them do some mock assessment centres with us as the candidates, as this will allow them to develop their skills in a safe environment and reduce the likelihood of making mistakes.

Finally, I would suggest undertaking an in-depth training needs analysis of these management roles as it is likely that there will be other areas of HR activity, which they don't feel comfortable with or don't have the skills to perform.

They may wish to undertake outside qualifications such as those the CIPD now offer in management and leadership but these needs should come out of the TNA.

*Answer 2*

Our current line managers need to upgrade their existing skills to be able to recruit and attract new key workers.

As the branches and line managers are geographically widespread any training we offer them will need to be computer based for the majority. I suggest that we research and buy in a recruitment e-learning package that is interactive that our managers can work through to gain the theory part of the training. They will need to cover how to advertise for staff in local media, how to attract the right candidate and how to sell the bank as a favoured employer. To test and review any current skills they have in recruiting staff when interviewing it would be advantageous to hold a workshop in each regional area which they can then pick up and develop their interview techniques through role play and feedback.

We could pilot this scheme in one area in the next two months and if successful roll it out to the whole organisation including lessons learnt from the pilot.

The first answer gained a distinction mark. It looks at the operational task of ensuring managers acquire the necessary skills, identifying some of the most important ones. Recognising the strategic importance of recruiting key workers for the bank, it also emphasises the need to ensure skills are fully developed and outlines a process whereby to reduce any errors. It then looks to the longer term and the need to ensure that managers are skilled not only in selection but also in all the HR tasks delegated to them.

The second answer gained a low pass mark for an adequate but narrowly focused approach that is only concerned with immediate operational needs. It proposes a sensible blended learning approach but does not identify the urgency or the strategic nature of the recruitment task. It ignores wider HR-related issues, but in its last sentence it does imply that in due course all managers need to be equipped with recruitment skills.

**Indicator 4: contribution to the retention of employees**

*Question 1*
*Identify one type of employee that your own organisation particularly needs to retain, and justify some L&D processes or initiatives that could aid their retention. (May 2003)*

This kind of question is open-ended so that candidates can propose any type of processes or initiatives, providing they convince the examiner that these would help to retain a valued type of employee. An emphasis on 'helping' is important, because L&D initiatives can only be supportive here. The state of the labour market, the daily actions of line management and the nature of HR strategies such as those to do with commitment and reward are also key influences on retention.

Here is an answer awarded a high distinction mark:

> As a manufacturing environment, the organisation relies heavily on specialised knowledge and experience. As the company developed from a very small operation to a medium sized enterprise in a very quick period of time, the skills base of the staff is not easily emulated. Due to the technical expertise required for a number of the machine operators' machines, a great deal of money and time has been spent on specialised machine training, often from international machine and training providers.
>
> Because the knowledge of staff represents a major source of competitive advantage, and given the level of training expenditure per operator, it is vital that these 'knowledge workers' are retained within the organisation.
>
> Processes and initiatives to aid the retention of these workers include:
> - Recognition of the value they add to the organisation, in the form of employee of the month schemes and bonus schemes.
> - Long-term career planning and clear progression paths that mark key points in their career.
> - Flexible working patterns particularly for younger employees. This affords staff the opportunity to devote time and knowledge to specific projects knowing that they can take time off at a later date.
> - Regular appraisals and personal development planning. This recognises objectives and allows the company the opportunity to assist the knowledge worker to strive to develop further knowledge and skills.

This response meets all the question's requirements and shows excellent BACKUP competencies. It discusses a specific type of employee in a well-described organisational context, it links career development with wider HR practice, it is equally strong in both its parts, and it is clearly presented.

## Question 2

**Outline and justify the advice you would give to an organisation intending to use an assessment centre for developmental purposes. (May 2004)**

The following 'thinking performer' response provides an example of a distinction-level answer to this question. It misses some of the key issues, cost-benefit assessment being the main omission, but it does emphasise the need for careful planning and for monitoring and evaluation. Its strength lies in its strategic thrust, its sensitivity to organisational context, and its business partner approach:

> 'x' (a named organisation) has just started using assessment centres to recruit staff with the right mix of skills, behaviour and knowledge to be promoted into the next grade. There has been a lot of (indecipherable) to do with this approach, so firstly you need to ensure that all staff are fully aware of the purpose of the assessment centre, what it is meant to do, how will it be run/managed, who will have responsibility, when will it start and where.
>
> You will need senior management buy in from the start as that is critical to the whole process. Senior managers must understand its aim and how they can help in the process, as must managers, as their buy in is key too, as they have the ultimate responsibility for identifying L&D needs, coaching, mentoring, appraising performance, etc. You also need to make sure that the staff who run the centre are well trained and have the right mixture of skills, knowledge and experience to run it and make effective decisions, and you need to manage staff expectations. It is not there to ensure promotion but is a tool to help and develop. So you need to pilot, monitor and evaluate and take the necessary steps for remedial action if necessary:
>
> Communicate, Inform, Consult, Benchmark, Network with other organisations to learn from what they found so as not to reinvent the wheel and ensure it fits in with the culture and structure of the organisation.

Typical of some answers that failed is one that merely produced two lists. One was headed 'Advantages', the other 'Disadvantages', the first containing five bullet points, the second three. Such answers are generalised, offer no advice as such, and often fail to show adequate understanding – in this case by not differentiating between assessment centres used for selection or promotion and those used for developmental purposes.

## Indicator 5: contribution to building organisational capacity and facilitating change

### Question I
**'The organisation of learning needs to be one of the key strategies discussed in the boardroom', said the CIPD's president at the 2002 Harrogate Conference. What is the rationale for this kind of claim? (May 2003)**

This question has a multiple focus, illustrating the way in which the L&D Standard's performance indicators are not about discrete functional tasks but about interconnected areas of activity.

At one level the question relates to Indicator 5. The rationale that Mike Kinsky (then CIPD president) provided for his claim was that organisations need people who can make their own distinctive contribution to their organisation in an increasingly uncertain world. The tool for achieving that is learning, so the organisation of learning needs to be a key corporate strategy (*People Management*, 7 November 2002, p7).

But this question also relates to Indicator 2, being to do with adding value through learning strategy. And because is it to do with strategic thinking and the sharing of valuable knowledge in the organisation it relates to Indicator 6 as well.

Here is an example of a type of answer that gained a pass, although not a high one:

> Learning and development has widely been recognised as a source of competitive advantage in organisations as it cannot be easily transferred and emulated. A recent *People Management* article entitled 'Ground force' (Sloman, June 2002) highlighted the need for L&D to be closely aligned to strategic objectives in order for L&D objectives to add value to the business.

It is vital that L&D strategies are discussed at board-room level in order to ensure that top management is committed to L&D as a key organisational process and that the key stakeholders recognise the need to make resources available to allow L&D initiatives to contribute to the long-term profitability of the company.

Such an answer tries to deal with the organisation of learning but does so only in the most generalised way, using an approach that is limited to the issue of strategic alignment of the Learning and Development process. For a higher grade it would need focus on learning in the organisation and how strategically valuable learning can be stimulated, shared and applied at all levels and in ways that add value. Some good answers also made links to wider HR practice in the organisation, especially that relating to resourcing and rewards.

### Question 2
*An L&D Unit has to make a substantial contribution to forthcoming organisational restructuring. The changes will involve some downsizing and also considerable reorganisation of people, jobs and new technology at workplace level. Propose and justify L&D activities to facilitate these changes. (November 2003)*

This question is to do with building organisational capacity and facilitating change. A merit or distinction answer would therefore incorporate the kinds of help suggested by the fifth performance indicator's Indicative Content 5.2 and 5.3.

One important cause of failure in this question was to produce little else than an outline of the systematic training cycle, as in the following answer:

L&D's contribution to an organisation's restructuring would first consist of communication with the board to agree strategy for L&D in the restructuring period. Once the need for training has been established:

- Propose objectives and strategy for the L&D activities required (for example, training in new software and in new roles, and refresher training to motivate and gain commitment to new structure).

- Determine profile of learning population.
- Agree strategy for new learning activities.
- Agree training specifications.
- Deliver, monitor and evaluate training.

Such an answer fails for a number of reasons. It suggests a process to follow in order to determine what training should be done, but it gives no information about the specific type of L&D activity that can aid restructuring in the situation outlined in the question. Its sketchy content and poor focus on the question suggest an ignorance about how L&D can facilitate that kind of change.

Compare that kind of approach with this answer, which gained full marks:

> First priority: L&D staff plus senior management team need to communicate new strategy and business objectives to all staff (explanation and justification of this step)
>
> Then a range of relevant training and learning activities:
> - Training in new skills (identifying training needs, target population, and appropriate ways of designing, delivering and evaluating training). There needs to be a special focus on multiskilling and IT skills.
> - Team working. Organise learning activities to enhance team-working and ensure technology maximises the spread of information here.
> - Performance management. Make sure there are clear guidelines in place about performance standards to be achieved after restructuring, with particular attention to L&D activities that can aid appraisal, induction into new roles and jobs, and the management of poor performance.
> - Career development. This is essential to aid leavers, to motivate and support those who are staying, and in particular to help and recognise managers involved in facilitating the whole change process.
> - Management development – especially for the new team leaders.
>
> In all this, essential to ensure that all L&D strategies are horizontally and vertically aligned.

This kind of answer focuses throughout on the specifics of the question. It is concise yet comprehensive and very well informed. It gains full marks for meeting all the criteria of a Master's-level answer.

## Indicator 6: stimulation of strategic awareness and development of knowledge

### Question 1
*Your chief executive officer often complains: 'there's too much hoarding of knowledge in this organisation'. What does your knowledge of wider organisational practice suggest might be the causes of this problem, and how do you think it could be tackled? (May 2003)*

Knowledge hoarding puts an organisation at risk because it reduces its capability to continuously improve and to radically innovate in products, processes and services. It also erects barriers to strategic awareness and the identification of strategic issues at all organisational levels. It thus damages competitive capability.

In answering a question like this you could draw on one or two of the articles that appear regularly in *People Management* and similar journals. Findings from a stream of research reports sponsored by the Institute have also illuminated this problem (see Appendix 1). Finally, knowledge drawn from your own knowledge of practice in a number of organisational settings would be perfectly acceptable providing that it is identified as such.

Here is an answer that was awarded a pass mark rather than a higher grade:

> A major reason for the hoarding of knowledge is the awareness of its unique value to the holder in maintaining their role and importance within the organisation. Staff often realise that their knowledge in conducting a specific task guarantees their job security and recognition within the company.
>
> In order to tackle this problem there must be a widespread change of culture towards one where the value of sharing knowledge is openly discussed and staff are recognised and rewarded for sharing knowledge that aids competitive advantage and the ultimate success of the business. Knowledge management should also be incorporated into the performance review of all staff and

managers to ensure its importance in adding value to the success of the company is further appreciated.

Such answers do show some understanding of individual causes of knowledge hoarding, but do not focus clearly enough on more significant organisational barriers. They echo a few of the most obvious findings from research, but only in a very generalised way. There is little demonstration of knowledge of good (or bad) organisational practice. Such answers also make some sensible suggestions about how to tackle knowledge hoarding, but they fail to make a clear distinction between the management of knowledge and stimulation of the whole knowledge process.

### Question 2
*It is often said that in today's competitive environment every employee needs to think more strategically about his or her own day to day work. Argue convincingly for one way by which to stimulate strategic thinking throughout your organisation. (May 2004)*

To show that an answer does not have to be lengthy or complex to gain a good mark, here is one that gained a distinction for a creative idea that, if implemented, seemed likely to make a real difference. Note how the candidate follows up the first suggestion with two sensible proposals to ensure managers' encouragement of strategic thinking in the workplace. This is a real example of a 'thinking performer' approach:

> At present, the strategic objectives of (named organisation) are not displayed on the front page of the Intranet, a tool which is used every day by all members of staff. I would suggest that this is altered so that they are, so that at all times people can see what they are working towards.
>
> However, I also think that a link should be attached to these objectives, so that employees can click to see these strategic objectives put into 'layman's' terms – sometimes the language used in vision/mission/strategy etc. can be difficult to understand, so if it was explained and put into context, all employees could see how they could apply this strategic thinking in their roles. This could be backed up with discussions with their line manager on a regular basis.

**Indicator 7: design and delivery of learning processes and activity**

*Question I*
*Identify from research or organisational practice with which you are familiar an example of excellent use of new electronically based technology in training or other kinds of learning activity, explaining why you think it is excellent. (November 2003)*

This question relates to the harnessing of new technology to L&D (Indicative Content 7.2). In order to gain a pass mark candidates had to both identify an example and explain why they saw it to be excellent. Purely descriptive answers to such questions cannot gain a pass. To convince that a practice is 'excellent' you must place it in context – hence the need to 'explain'.

As interesting contrasts, one answer to this question described a modest use of fairly standard e-based training technology in a small firm, yet assessed so thoughtfully its rationale, its impact on the organisation, and the steps being taken to continuously improve it from tentative beginnings that the candidate gained a high mark. Another answer described the highly sophisticated use of e-learning in a big, wealthy high-tech organisation, but left the reader to assume this was 'excellent'. There was no attempt to justify the claim, and in reality the firm seemed to be doing not so much what was 'excellent' as what was the norm for its type and sector. It also had every resource needed at its disposal. That answer failed because of its lack of reflective and evaluative quality. It was not that of a thinking performer.

Here is a type of answer that just scraped through:

> My employer has two very effective learning tools that are outstanding for a small to medium sized firm, providing the workforce with exceptional learning vehicles.
>
> First, the company Internet. Everyone can gain information from it via their workstation, from the Company Handbook to various Noticeboard papers. Employees can find out about other staff, share knowledge, discuss past training experiences and chat about work-related activities. Training feedback is done through the intranet and this enables anonymity in order to encourage honest views.

Second, a specially designed training package, which doubles as a testing package for selection purposes. This allows people to train or test a variety of e-based systems and enables a clear understanding of results.

There are a number of reasons why such an answer gains only a marginal pass. It convinces as drawing on a real-life situation, but it has little evaluative content to support its claim of 'excellence' for the chosen approaches, which in fact seem fairly unremarkable. The reader is told nothing about the before–after situation relating to the approaches. There is no information about any cost-benefit analysis or assessment of important but non-quantifiable measures such as improved selection, retention, e-technology skills or motivation of employees. Finally, the answer discusses two initiatives but the question asked only for one. That requirement was intended to encourage answers with more depth than achieved in this one.

### Question 2
*Over coffee, one of your Personnel colleagues says to you: 'I've just read that it's out of date to base the design of learning events on the systematic training model. What do you think?' Provide an informed response. (May 2004)*

Several writers have made this claim, including Sloman (2001). This kind of question requires candidates to have a sound knowledge of theory coupled with good analytical skill. Here is an answer that just scraped through:

I would have to say I don't agree it's out of date to base the design of learning events on the systematic training model. Ultimately there are views on many subjects but CIPD, PSLB, Harrison and TSLB support basing design on the model. I would imagine that in designing any learning event you should look at it fairly systematically:
- what is needed?
- who are the audience/profile?
- depth of subject/objectives
- design

- delivery
- monitor/evaluate
- review.

In order to ensure the training fits you need to establish who and what, and following design and delivery based on the above you need to ensure it was worthwhile.

Why did this basic answer gain a pass? Not because my name was mentioned in it! It was because it gave a direct response to the question in the first sentence; it then cited authoritative sources of support for the model by referring to the CIPD and the old Personnel and Training Standards Lead Bodies (something very few candidates noted); it showed an awareness of the systematic model, even if sketchy; and it emphasised the value of the model in helping to ensure good fit in training design – an important point.

## Indicator 8: evaluation and assessment of L&D outcomes and investment

### Question 1
*You are a consultant, helping a small firm to review the outcomes of its training activity over the past couple of years so that it can decide whether it should appoint a full-time training officer or continue its policy of combining part-time help with reliance on its personnel generalist. What kind of information will you seek in your evaluation task, and why? (November 2003)*

This question is concerned with the overall payback the organisation in question has achieved from its past L&D investment (Indicative Content 8.3), and with the data and information sources that the consultant should tap into in order to help resolve the staffing issue (Indicative Content 8.4).

For a pass, making a few sensible recommendations about 'what kind of information?' is enough, but any answer should relate 'kind of information' to the staffing issue, not simply to evaluating past L&D activity. Answers that were knowledgeable about how to assess organisational outcomes of L&D activity and were well contextualised gained a merit or distinction. Here is a type of answer not quite worth a pass:

> *Information to evaluate:*
> - Establish the cost of external compared with internal provision. Could the outputs have been achieved to the same level but more cheaply? This business focus on the issues is essential.
> - Use Kirkpatrick's evaluation model (outlined by the candidate) to assess how much of a contribution training activities have made in the past to the achievement of business objectives.
> - Find out the added value of those activities. Would a dedicated L&D practitioner have been better able to plan and organise training than a generalist personnel practitioner?

Such an answer relates quite well to part of the context in the question. However it does not contain any reference to the need to also seek information on likely future training and development needs. It is only concerned with the past, and it makes no reference to the small firm scenario.

### Question 2
*You work in a medium-sized organisation. Show your knowledge of wider organisational practice or published research in your response to the following email from your chief executive officer: 'I've just got back from a conference on 'Managing organisational learning' where I heard a lot about corporate universities. Could we use one here?' (May 2004)*

This question is about calculating the 'pay forward' of an organisation's investment in learning activity. It could also be interpreted as relating to the seventh indicator, in so far as it concerns design of learning initiatives, and to the second indicator because of its value-adding implications.

Consider the following answer:

> Corporate universities have been present within major organisations for many years, e.g., McDonalds, and have proved to be highly effective within particular environments e.g. very large employee numbers, wide geographical area, extensive financial resources.

These circumstances are potentially not applicable to a medium sized organisation. They require a lot of time taken by 'students' to complete the courses which could have negative impact on an organisation of this size.

Success rates for 'corporate universities' tend to be very high and the knowledge imported is excellent for achieving strategic goals, however my opinion is we would simply be creating highly skilled, highly (indecipherable) managers who are likely to leave an organisation of this size for one with greater employment prospects, e.g. GE. We would be left with a large investment that may serve to have minimum effect on the strategic capability of our business.

This was awarded a marginal fail. It does not give the questioner any idea of what a corporate university is, and in fact could refer to almost any type of strategically-focused L&D initiative. This means that its 'advice' is not meaningful. Also it does not offer any way forward, simply dismissing the idea out of hand on unconvincing grounds.

By contrast the following answer gained a pass:

Corporate universities like those used in Barclays and Lloyds TSB have their strengths in as much as they provide a range of generic and bespoke courses to very different business units operating in diverse environments. Retail Branch Banking operates in a relatively stable low staff turnover environment whereas Contact Centres operate in a high turnover environment.

The corporate university therefore utilises economies of scale by offering courses e.g. Diversity, Influencing, Performance Development as generic courses bringing together employees from all different sectors of the organisation.

Secondly the Corporate University actively promotes organisational learning through its corporate brand and promotion through its own website.

The Corporate University provides a centralised service provision of training and as with Barclays through to Metro Centres it provides learning outside of working hours for both employees and their families (on weekends) promoting and cementing employee engagement.

However corporate universities are very expensive to run though essentially the idea of a corporate university is to provide centralised training available to all staff. An extension of the training services provides is to enhance the use of (indecipherable) learning and facilitate learning activities in a similar way that LearnDirect promote lifelong learning.

There are a number of options from a full range of corporate trainers providing centralised generic and business unit bespoke courses to a website portal to e-learning activities.

This answer gives a fair idea of what a corporate university can do, although it never clearly differentiates it from, for example, a learning resource or training centre. It tends to be repetitive and is primarily a description of benefits. Still, it does contain some relevant advice and overall is competent enough to pass.

Finally, here is an answer typical of a number that gained either full or very high marks for their combination of information, focus on every aspect of the question and meaningful advice:

Corporate universities are more commonly associated with major blue chip companies. For example, BAE Systems operate a corporate university throughout their company which is a major employer in the aerospace and shipbuilding sectors. But they employ over 100,000 people.

We are a medium sized company and we really need to conduct a full investment appraisal with integrated cost–benefit analysis before we embark on this road.

We may be better off considering an alternative, such as Learning Resource Centres (LRCs). Barclays Bank uses this approach and has successfully formed LRCs at their major employing locations.

Corporate universities generally use both internal resources and an external business partner from the academic world as part of their generic approach.

We also need to think about how we define organisational learning, how we want to manage knowledge within the company and whether we wish to commit ourselves publicly to becoming a Learning Organisation. However, even after analysis there are still a number of options open to us without committing our company to the major investment and overhead of a corporate university.

Critics of existing corporate universities argue that this is just LRCs dressed up in a fancy title. For example Ashridge Management Centre operate a very complex and attractive LRDC with many ex-students still connected via a membership scheme. Given a choice, I would prefer to join such a well-organised and effective arrangement rather than link to a 'corporate university' which was more an image trip rather than a university in substance.

On balance, my advice is to work out the numbers first, and conduct an assessment of our needs including benchmarking with our peer group companies before introducing a corporate university for our firm. We may, of course, be able in the final evaluation to be able to combine our resources with other companies to create one as an option.

## Indicator 9: role and tasks of the ethical practitioner

### Question I
*'Ethics and professionalism – as far as we L&D specialists are concerned they both boil down to the same thing, don't they?' asks a colleague over coffee. Outline a convincing reply. (May 2003)*

This question asks candidates to express a view on the connection between ethics and professionalism, both of which form an integral part of the L&D Standard.

One way of responding to the statement would be to take a fairly neutral stance by defining the two terms and briefly discussing the interaction between the two. Another way would be to come down firmly on one side or the other when responding to the colleague's statement. A 'no' or a 'yes' answer would be equally acceptable if well argued. For example:

A *'No, they don't'* response can be found in the core text in Chapter 7. Such an answer would need to clearly distinguish between ethics and professionalism, the former involving some kind of moral stance by practitioners, the latter the exercise of a consistently reliable and high level of expertise in a defined field of knowledge and skills. High marks would go to answers with a practical twist, showing how 'ethics' raises a variety of issues to do with promotion of and access to learning opportunities, and with the design, delivery and evaluation of training and of other L&D processes.

A *'Yes, in a way they do'* response would tend to take ethics for granted as an integral part of any professional's code of practice and would probably interpret it as being basically about legal compliance and a generalised concern for fair treatment. Not as convincing an answer, perhaps, but worthy of a pass if well argued, and of more than that if accompanied by a practical illustration relevant to the L&D field.

### Question 2
**Outline a convincing reply to this email from an L&D colleague who works in another organisation:**
**'Hi! I want to introduce some short training courses for line managers who have just been handed L&D responsibilities following our recent restructuring. It occurs to me that in addition to the usual stuff maybe I should put in something about ethics in relation to L&D. Only I'm a bit vague on that one. Any ideas, please?' (November 2003)**

This question again concerns ethical issues related to L&D activity. At pass level markers looked for answers that made a fair attempt to give meaning to the term 'ethics' and that raised a few important ethical points that anyone with L&D responsibilities should consider.

Some candidates discussed ethics without any reference to L&D activity. Many forgot to relate their advice to a scenario of recent organisational restructuring but providing they responded well to other contextual aspects of the question this was overlooked. Here is one answer that, while not explicitly mentioning restructuring, was so exceptional in its depth and quality in all other respects that it gained almost full marks:

> As part of short training courses for managers there are some key points that should be covered. There are a number of theories about ethics, as well as various definitions, but essentially

ethics is about bringing the greatest benefit to the most people within an organisation.

From a line manager's perspective ethics can simply be described as:

- No one being treated unjustifiably less favourably than anyone else.
- No activity should make things worse for any single individual, albeit that not all people might receive exactly the same benefits.

Line managers therefore need to be made aware of two issues:

- Diversity: that is, the treatment of people as individuals in ways that value their differences.
- discrimination legislation: which states that to achieve legal compliance no one can must be discriminated against unfairly on grounds of sex, race, gender, ethnicity or disability (by December 2003), religious beliefs or sexual orientation.

From an L&D perspective line managers therefore need to ensure that they are offering equal training opportunities to everyone (keeping records to demonstrate this and to have a defence against claims of unfair/unlawful discrimination). They also need to consider how this can be achieved across a diverse workforce (e.g. part-time workers, different ethnic groups, or even those with different learning styles from a desired 'norm'). Considering alternative learning methods for part-time workers is particularly important since they may be unable to attend full-day training or courses involving overnight residence.

Some company approaches in the L&D field for line managers to consider include the following:

- Ford has set up diversity discussion groups to encourage sharing of beliefs and values.
- M&S has used union learning reps. to provide training in English as a second language.
- BT has a female networking group to encourage career development as well as a 'Be Able' group (for disabled workers) and a 'Kaleidoscope' group (for gay/lesbian/bi-sexual workers). These groups are intended to achieve employee engagement, give members a group voice and get feedback on marketing information and product knowledge.

**Indicator 10: continuing professional self-development**

*Question 1*
*As a newly qualified CIPD professional, you want to improve your L&D knowledge and ability even though you are working in a Human Resource function where there are as yet no opportunities for you to specialise in L&D. Outline and justify up to three steps you could take to achieve that improvement. (May 2003)*

This question focuses on continuing professional self-development but also relates to the L&D Standard as a whole. It was designed as a very open one that could give every candidate a chance to be creative.

Typical steps cited in answers included:

- volunteering to take on some value-adding L&D tasks

- shadowing a L&D specialist

- seeking involvement in project work with a L&D dimension

- delivering some input into an induction programme, thereby working alongside L&D staff in a L&D event

- reading specialist L&D literature and accessing L&D websites

- going to CIPD branch meetings, and various seminars, conferences and so on that focus on L&D topics

- seeking out an L&D mentor.

To gain a pass it was not enough to give a list or a description of steps. There had to be a convincing justification of proposals, both by reference to their relevance and to their feasibility. Answers reflecting on likely benefits that candidates would achieve for the organisation as well as for him/herself were awarded high marks for demonstrating thinking performer and business partner qualities.

*Question 2*
*You want to get actively involved in some external networks (other than those relating to the CIPD) and/or local initiatives in order both to enhance your professional development and to bring benefit to your organisation. Identify two such networks/initiatives and provide reasons for their choice. (May 2004)*

Among the many very good answers to this question, more than one gained full marks for thoughtful and excellently justified choices. The answer below is impressive because of the attention the candidate has given not only to explaining the initiative (first paragraph) and the network (second paragraph) chosen, but to convincing the reader that these choices would be feasible. The evaluative content of answers like these fully meets master's level criteria.

As this is my first positioning in an HR environment, as part of my continuing professional development and to add value to my company I think it would be beneficial for me to approach an independent HR consultant to 'Shadow' for a week in order to gain HR knowledge in a broader organisational context than just for the organisation I currently work for. I have already approached such a consultant who has agreed to this, and this was through networking at a local legal firm's 'breakfast seminars' which not only keep me up to date but also enable me to meet others with whom I can develop relationships to mutual benefit. It will help my company as I will have a wider appreciation of what happens in other organisations. A week is not a long time to achieve a huge amount of knowledge or experience, but it will help and will also enable me to build on a wider network of contacts.

Another means is to attend local Chamber of Commerce networking events, whether these are in a social setting such as an evening meal and skittles or a breakfast seminar which usually has keynote speakers who focus on current 'hot topics'. This is an excellent way to develop links with other organisations and I can pass leads onto my colleagues who can in turn approach them to do business. As I am not a sales person, then contacts see me in a non-threatening way, in a neutral environment and are more likely to be seen as personal friendships rather than business contacts. It would also be useful for the organisation and myself in sourcing new recruits to fill vacant positions, which is a difficult task in the current climate.

# Conclusion

The main purpose of this chapter has been to provide a selection of questions typifying those that can be expected in the PDS Generalist L&D examinations and to offer advice on how to tackle them. I started the chapter with some advice on how to reach Master's-level standard in the L&D examination.

The questions have been listed under the L&D performance indicators to which they primarily relate. Like several other texts on learning and development/human resource development, my own CIPD core text contains many more examples of the kind of questions relevant for those studying for internally assessed as well as nationally assessed CIPD examinations. Ways of answering those questions are suggested by material covered in each chapter and in the tutors' online manual available for those using *Learning and development* as a core text on their programmes.

In offering guidelines for answers I have incorporated information that can help you expand your current understanding of the L&D Standard's 10 performance indicators on which the questions are focused. To give as much help as possible I have included a number of examples of types of answers given by past candidates and have explained how they were assessed.

# SECTION 4

## CONCLUSION

# 5 CONCLUSION

## Using the revision guide

This guide has offered practical advice to those of you who are preparing to take examinations in the Learning and Development Generalist field.

**In Section 1,** Chapter 1, I have outlined the framework of the CIPD's Professional Development Scheme (PDS), discussed the concepts and competencies that justify its qualifications being officially recognised as at Master's level, and suggested ways of tackling PDS-type examination papers.

**In Section 2** I have explained (Chapter 2) the CIPD's Learning and Development (L&D) Generalist Standard, and the criteria against which L&D examination candidates are assessed. In Chapter 3 I have reflected on questions frequently asked about that examination.

**In Section 3,** Chapter 4, I have provided a range of past L&D examination questions and explained how they relate to the L&D Standard's performance indicators. I have followed each question by suggestions on how it might be tackled in order to achieve a master's level standard of performance. Illustrations taken from past candidates' answers have, I hope, brought this vital chapter fully to life.

It is now in your hands to relate the advice in this guide to all the other knowledge gained through your wider reading, your course of study and your daily work experience. Your final task is to apply that entire body of knowledge to the examination situation.

## Doing well on the day

Here is some advice to bear in mind on the day of your examination:

1.  Use your 10-minute reading time mainly to absorb the Section A information, but leave enough time to go through the Section B questions and make a careful choice of seven to answer.

2. With regard to your case study reading time:
   - Read carefully through the whole case, and focus on the tasks set by the examiner. If you do not respond clearly to those tasks you cannot gain a pass in Section A.
   - As you read, get to grips with the organisation's external environment, the kind of progress it is making in achieving its business goals, and any problems, opportunities and challenges that it is encountering (with their likely causes). This will give you the vital business framework to which you should always relate your case study answers.
   - Try to understand the internal organisational context that influences people's commitment and performance. The 'Black Box' research (Purcell *et al* 2003; Hutchinson and Purcell 2003) demonstrates the importance of top management's vision, mission and leadership, front line managers' behaviour and HR strategies and practices in shaping that context and in releasing the commitment, skills and discretionary behaviour across the workforce that can produce above-average organisational performance.
   - Establish what is factual and what is not in the case study information. Your conclusions need to rest on an adequately solid base of evidence. Likewise identify any important areas of incomplete information in the study. In real life those areas would call for further fact-finding before making decisions about them.

3. In responding to Section B questions, remember that quality counts much more than quantity. PDS candidates in the L&D examination produce about three quarters of a page on average in response to each of their chosen Section B answers. However, this is only an average. Many candidates produce more, some less. Some write lengthy answers yet fail because those answers are poorly informed, are not to the point or have some other critical weakness. Others write adequate answers that are quite brief.

4. Remember that no script can be perfect. One of the weakest answers included in Section B feedback in this chapter was written by a candidate who also provided one of the best. Their

script ended up as a strong pass. As in examinations so in life, one or two weaknesses rarely kill!

And that leads to the last FAQ:

**Am I likely to pass my PDS examinations?**

'Yes', if you convince the examiners that you understand and can explain enough to practise in the professional fields that the examinations cover. Remember that the ability to quote from textbooks or outline theory is never enough. You must use theory in ways that are practical, value-adding and well tailored to a given scenario. In Chapter 4, I identified six ways in which to reach a master's level standard in your examination performance. I repeat them here:

1. Deal with complex issues systematically and creatively.

2. Make sound judgements in the absence of complete data.

3. Show originality in tackling and solving problems.

4. Demonstrate competence to plan and advise on how to implement tasks at your professional level.

5. Propose/make convincing, feasible and ethical decisions in complex and unpredictable situations.

6. Communicate your conclusions clearly to your audience.

## The experiential learning cycle

This concludes the cycle of activity covered by the guide. The cycle started with an explanation of the PDS and the philosophy underpinning it. It continued with a reflection on the L&D Standard and the performance indicators against which examination candidates are assessed. It then moved into the L&D examination itself, exploring its basis and coverage. Finally it provided many past PDS examination questions for you to test yourself against, and feedback to aid your future performance.

If this process has a ring of familiarity it is because it exemplifies the experiential learning cycle pictured in Figure 1. It is a fitting model with which to end this Guide.

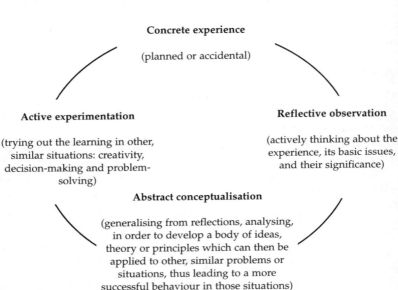

**Concrete experience**

(planned or accidental)

**Active experimentation**

(trying out the learning in other, similar situations: creativity, decision-making and problem-solving)

**Reflective observation**

(actively thinking about the experience, its basic issues, and their significance)

**Abstract conceptualisation**

(generalising from reflections, analysing, in order to develop a body of ideas, theory or principles which can then be applied to other, similar problems or situations, thus leading to a more successful behaviour in those situations)

**Figure 1** The experiential cycle of learning (based on Kolb, Rubin and McIntyre, 1974)

Source: Harrison (2000) p239

# APPENDIX I

## Recent CIPD research publications related to the L&D field, and CIPD research information sources

### Learning and development – general

REYNOLDS, J., CALEY, L. and MASON, R. (2002) *How do people learn?* Research report.
SLOMAN, M. and ROLPH, J. (2003) *E-learning: the learning curve.* 'Change Agenda' *series.*

### Training, learning and development – national policy and trends

*Reflections: new developments in training: experts' views on the 2004 training and development survey findings.* (2004)
STEWART, J. and TANSLEY, C. (2002) *Training in the Knowledge Economy.* Research report.
*Trade Union Learning Representatives.* 'Change Agenda' series. (2004)
WILSON, D., LANK, E., WESTWOOD, A., KEEP, E., LEADBEATER, C. and SLOMAN, M. (2001) *The future of learning for work.* Executive briefing.
*Workplace learning in Europe.* (2001) Report on a CIPD European Workplace Learning Seminar, London.

### Knowledge management/the knowledge economy

BEAUMONT, P.B. and HUNTER, L.C. (2002). *Managing knowledge workers: the HR dimension.* Research report.
SCARBROUGH, H. and CARTER, C. (2000) *Investigating knowledge management.* Research report.
SKAPINKER, M. (2002) *Knowledge management.* 'Change Agenda' series.
SWART, J., KINNIE, N. and PURCELL, J. (2003) *People and performance in knowledge-intensive firms: a comparison of six research and technology organisations.* Research report.

## Strategising and organising

BREWSTER, C., HARRIS, H. and SPARROW, P. (2002) *Globalising HR.* Executive briefing.

*Reorganising for Success: CEOs' and HR managers' perceptions.* Survey report. (2003).

WHITTINGTON, R. and MAYER, M. (2002) *Organising for success in the Twenty-First Century: a starting point for change.* Research report.

### The people–performance link

CIPD and THE MANUFACTURERS' ORGANISATION. (2004) *Maximising employee potential and business performance.*

GUEST, D.E. and CONWAY, N. (2001).*Employer perceptions of the psychological contract.* Research report.

HUTCHINSON, S. and PURCELL, J. (2003) *Bringing policies to life: the vital role of front line managers in people management.* Executive briefing.

*Performance through people: the new people management.* 'Change Agenda' series. (2001).

PURCELL, J., KINNIE, N., HUTCHINSON, S., RAYTON, B. and SWART, J. (2003) *Understanding the people and performance link: unlocking the black box.* Research report.

SCARBROUGH, H. and ELIAS, J. (2002) *Evaluating human capital.* Research report.

### Access to above and similar sources of information

*CIPD surveys.* Findings can be viewed and downloaded from www.cipd.co.uk/surveys.

*CIPD research reports* are quite expensive products that are available from CIPD Publishing and are not always stocked in college or university libraries. However, summaries of all the reports are available on www.cipd.co.uk/researchsummaries

Four regular publications by the CIPD should also be noted here:

- The quarterly publication *Impact* provides a regular update on CIPD policy and research activities (www.cipd.co.uk/impact).

- The annual *Overview of CIPD surveys* does a similar job in relation to all the Institute's surveys.

- The occasional series *Perspectives* offers essays to improve understanding of, and stimulate discussion on, issues of general interest to and beyond the profession.

- 'Change Agendas' are forward-thinking essays by leading authorities on a variety of key topics such as people and public sector reform. Visit them at www.cipd.co.uk/changeagendas.

The website www.cipd.co.uk/research also advises when articles on the details of CIPD-sponsored research have appeared in *People Management* and when press releases have come out, as well as providing links to presentations the CIPD's Professional Knowledge Advisers have given around the country.

The 'training community' area of CIPD's website is a useful way to find out information and exchange views, ideas and experiences ( www.cipd.co.uk/communities).

Finally, the CIPD provides new online, downloadable tools developed from its research, as part of its work of turning its research findings into practical, relevant material for its members. www.cipd.co.uk/tools offers checklists, diagnostics and good-practice frameworks like 'Planning the implementation of e-learning'.

# REFERENCES

BEAUMONT, P. and HUNTER, L. (2002) *Managing knowledge workers: the HRM dimension.* Research report. London: Chartered Institute of Personnel and Development (CIPD).

BREWSTER, C., HARRIS, H. and SPARROW, P. (2002) *Globalising HR.* Executive briefing. London: CIPD.

CIPD (2001a) *Workplace learning in Europe.* Report on a CIPD European Workplace Learning Seminar. London: CIPD.

CIPD (2001b) *Performance through people: the new people management.* 'Change Agenda' series. London: CIPD.

CIPD (2003) *Reorganising for success: CEOs' and HR managers' perceptions.* Survey report. London: CIPD.

CIPD (2004a) *Training and development 2004: survey report.* London: CIPD.

CIPD (2004b) *Trade union learning representatives.* 'Change Agenda' series. London: CIPD.

CIPD (2004c) *Reflections: new developments in training: experts' views on the 2004 training and development survey findings.* London: CIPD.

CIPD and THE MANUFACTURERS' ORGANISATION. (2004) *Maximising employee potential and business performance.* London: CIPD.

GUEST, D.E. and CONWAY, N. (2001) *Employer perceptions of the psychological contract.* Research report. London: CIPD.

HARRISON, R. (2000) *Employee development.* 2nd edn. London: CIPD.

HARRISON, R. (2002a) *Learning and development.* 3rd edn. London: CIPD.

HARRISON, R. (2002b) *Learning and development: tutors on-line manual.* London: CIPD. Online version available at: http://www.cipd.co.uk/

HARRISON, R. and KESSELS, J. (2003) *Human resource development in a knowledge economy: an organisational view.* Basingstoke: Palgrave Macmillan.

HUTCHINSON, S. and PURCELL, J. (2003). *Bringing policies to life: the vital role of front line managers in people management.* Executive briefing. London: CIPD.

JAMES, R. (2004) 'How to get managers' buy-in for training'. *People Management*, Vol. 10, No. 6. pp52–53.

KING, Z. (2003) *Career management: a guide*. London: CIPD.

KOLB, D.A., RUBIN, I.M. and MCINTYRE, J.M. (1974) *Organizational psychology: an experiential approach*. Englewood Cliffs, NJ: Prentice Hall.

MARCHINGTON, M. and WILKINSON, A. (2002) *People management and development: human resource management at work*. 2nd edn. London: CIPD.

MAYO, A. (1998) *Creating a training and development strategy*. London: Institute of Personnel and Development (IPD).

PURCELL, J., KINNIE, N., HUTCHINSON, S., RAYTON, B. and SWART, J. (2003) *Understanding the people and performance link: unlocking the black box*. Research report. London: CIPD.

REID, M. A., BARRINGTON, H. and BROWN, M. (2004) *Human resource development*. 7th edn. London: CIPD.

REYNOLDS, J., CALEY, L. and MASON, R. (2002) *How do people learn?* Research report. London: CIPD.

SCARBROUGH, H. and CARTER, C. (2000) *Investigating knowledge management*. Research report. London: CIPD.

SCARBROUGH, H. and ELIAS, J. (2002) *Evaluating human capital*. Research report. London: CIPD.

SCARBROUGH, H. and SWAN, J. (eds). (1999) *Case studies in knowledge management*. London: IPD.

SKAPINKER, M. (2002) *Knowledge management*. 'Change Agenda' series. London: CIPD.

SLOMAN, M. (2001) 'Hardier laurels please'. *People Management*, Vol. 7, No. 25. p39.

SLOMAN, M. (2002) 'Ground force'. *People Management*, Vol. 8, No.13. pp42–46.

SLOMAN, M. (2003) *Training in the age of the learner*. London: CIPD.

SLOMAN, M. and ROLPH, J. (2003) *E-learning: the learning curve*. 'Change agenda' series. London: CIPD.

STEWART, J. (2004) *Employee development practice*. Harlow: Financial Times/Prentice Hall.

STEWART, J. and TANSLEY, C. (2002) *Training in the knowledge economy:* Research report. London: CIPD.

SWART, J., KINNIE, N. and PURCELL, J. (2003) *People and performance in knowledge-intensive firms*. Research report. London: CIPD.

WALTON, J. (1999) *Strategic human resource development*. Essex: Pearson Education.

WHITTINGTON, R. and MAYER, M. (2002) *Organising for success in the twenty-first century: a starting point for change.* Research report. London: CIPD.

WILSON, D., LANK, E., WESTWOOD, A., KEEP, E., LEADBEATER, C. and SLOMAN, M. (2001) *The future of learning for work.* Executive briefing. London: CIPD.

# INDEX

**A**

action plan/action planning, 7, 36, 52

answers *see* questions and answers

Ashridge Management Centre, 77

**B**

BACKUP framework, xiii, 4, 5–6, 42, 43, 64

Beaumont, P. B., 23

'big issue(s)', 15, 17–28

bite-sized training, 50

'Black Box' research, 30, 86

business partner, 4–5, 11, 24, 25–6, 30, 42, 58–60, 65

**C**

*Career management: a guide*, 21

CIPD research resources, 9, 24, 37, 45, 54, 56, 90, 91

  publications, 9, 10, 18, 23, 27, 30, 31, 34, 37, 66, 69, 90

competencies

  application capability, 4, 5, 22

  broad understanding, 5, 6

  business orientation, 5

  presentation skills, 6, 7, 17, 31, 42, 43

  *see also* key competencies; knowledge/performance indicators

  consistency, 23–4, 30

context, organisational, 4, 6, 7, 109, 17, 28, 42, 86

corporate universities, 74–7

*Creating a training and development strategy*, 18, 34

culture

  learning, 32, 70

  organisational, 15, 21–2, 25, 26–7, 32, 48–51, 69

cycle of activity, 24, 60, 67

  experiential learning cycle, 87

**D**

development

  continuous, 27–8

  self, 27–8

  *see also* Professional Development Scheme

discrimination, 62, 79, 80

diversity, 5, 26, 29, 76, 79

downsizing, 43, 57, 67–8

**E**

e-learning, 50, 57, 62, 71, 76

*Employee development practice*, 8, 23, 27

Employment Protection Act, 31

environment

  business, 6, 15, 46, 56

  learning, 22, 48

ethics

  and professionalism, 77–8

  *see also* key competencies, ethics

evaluation, 7, 36
  *see also* examiners,
    expectations; questions
    and answers
examinations *see* examiners;
  generalist examinations;
  questions and answers
examiners, 29, 38
  expectations of, 6, 10–11, 19,
    21–2, 28, 31, 35–6, 48–9, 56,
    58, 59, 73, 78
experiential, *see* cycle of
  experiential learning

**F**
FAQs, 8–11, 29–38, 87
flexibility, 7, 47, 51

**G**
generalist examinations, 6–8,
  9–10, 29–38
  common questions about *see*
    FAQs
  exam tactics, 85–7
  expertise needed for, 31–2
  preparing for, 24–5, 36–7
  Section A, 6–7, 9–10, 17, 18,
    19, 21–2, 35, 42, 43–51, 85,
    86
  Section B, 7, 10–11, 17, 38, 42,
    43, 51–81, 85, 86
  questions, need to read, 7, 8,
    10, 11, 73, 86
  weighting/marks, 9–10, 37–8,
    55, 61, 73–4
  *see also* research; questions
    and answers

**H**
Harrison, R., xi, xiii, 15, 20, 21,
  23, 27, 29, 34, 48, 72
*How do people learn?*, 23
human resource
  strategy/ies, 34
  practice/s, 10, 15
*Human resource development in
  a knowledge economy*, 27, 82
Hunter, L. C., 23
Hutchinson, S., 34, 61, 86

**I**
*Impact*, 9, 90
indicative content, 16, 37, 54, 59,
  68, 71, 74
internal assessment, ix, 49, 82
information technology, 44,
  49–50, 68, 70, 71–2
  *see also* CIPD research
    resources; e-learning
integration/integrating/
  integrative
  horizontal, 34–5, 59, 68
  of L&D, 33, 34–5, 59, 68
  vertical, 34–5, 59, 68

**J**
James, R., 30

**K**
Kessels, J., 23, 27
key competencies
  1. integration of learning
    and needs 17, 18, 26, 33,
    34–5, 47, 54–7, 59
  2. providing a value-adding
    L&D function, 5, 17, 19,

34, 35, 45–50 *passim*, 57–60
*passim*, 66, 67, 74–7
3. contributing to recruit-
ment/management
processes, 19–20, 60–3
4. contribution to employee
retention, 20–1, 63–6
5. contribution to capacity
building, 21–2, 26, 29, 30,
66–9
6. stimulation of awareness
and development, 22–3,
66–7, 69–70
7. design and delivery of
L&D, 23–4, 58–60, 71–3
8. evaluation of L&D, 24–5,
31–2, 57–60, 73–7
9. ethics, 5, 26–7, 42–3, 77–9
10. ensuring continued self-
development, 27–8, 80–1
Kinsky, M., 66
knowledge
explicit, 22
management, 22
tacit, 22
knowledge indicators *see*
performance/knowledge
indicators
knowledge, xiv, 4–9 *passim*, 18,
21, 26, 29–34 *passim*, 37, 42,
48, 51, 54, 56, 59, 64, 69–70,
72, 74, 85
developing, 22, 29, 34, 48,
69–70, 81
hoarding, 69–70
sharing, 5, 22, 23, 24, 66, 71
updating, 7, 8–9, 37

**L**
learning and development (L&D)
defined, 29–30
and downsizing, 57, 67–8
and e-learning, 57
roles, 15–16
Standard, xi, 16, 29, 36, 37, 41,
66, 77, 80, 82, 85, 87
language of vision statements, 70
Learning and Development
Generalist Standard, 15–28
holistic approach, 16, 31
*see also* generalist examinations; performance
indicators
*Learning and Development*, xi, 15,
82
*Learning and development
resource book*, 18
learning reps *see* trade unions
learning resource centres
(LRCs), 76, 77
lifelong learning, 54–5, 76
line managers/management, 25,
30, 35, 56, 61–3, 79

**M**
MALPAS, 18
management, 21, 24, 27, 32, 33, 70
career, xi, 20
development, xi, 20, 66
knowledge, 22, 69–70, 76
performance, xi, 17, 19–20,
50, 60–3, 68
processes, 19–20
Marchington, M., 23
Marks and Spencer, 33, 50, 79
Master's level, 3–6

achieving, xiii–xiv, 20, 28, 42–3, 69, 81, 85, 87
defined, 3–4
Mayo, A., 18, 34

**N**
national vocational education and training (NVET), 18

**O**
organisation strategy, 4
organisational
  culture, 15, 21–2, 25, 26–7, 32, 48–51, 69
  learning, 26, 32, 48, 75, 76
  practice, 4, 8, 42, 45, 47, 50, 51, 54, 56–8, 69–70, 71–2, 75–6
  vision, 15, 22, 47

**P**
pay-forward, 75
*People management*, 9, 10, 30, 31, 37, 66, 69
performance/knowledge indicators, xi, 15, 16, 17–28, 36, 41, 51, 60, 66, 82, 85, 87
  *see also* key competencies
performance management, 17, 19–20, 51, 60–1, 69
personnel and development (P&D), 5, 6, 44–5
  achieving goals, 5
  development plans, 49–50
PQS examinations, xiii, xiv
Premier Care, 18, 22, 43–51
problem-solving, 6
professional development, continuing, 27–8, 48, 80–1

Professional Development Scheme (PDS), 3–6
  assessment criteria, 6
  difference from PQS, xiii–xiv
Professional Standards, 1–11
professionalism, 27, 28, 77–8
Purcell, J., 20, 30, 33, 34, 61, 86

**Q**
questions and answers
  good/excellent answers, 20, 25–6, 28, 31, 32, 46–8, 51–3, 55–7, 59–60, 62–3, 64, 65, 68–9, 70–1, 73–4, 76–81
  length of answers, 86
  questions, need to read, 7, 8, 10, 11, 73, 86
  strategy for answers, 37, 42–3, 48–9, 51–2, 56, 60–1, 63–4, 67, 68, 71–4 *passim*, 77–8, 80
  typical/average answers, 34–5, 36, 49–50, 69–70, 75–6, 80
  typical questions, 18, 20, 21, 22, 27, 28, 43–4
  weak answers, 7, 21, 28, 45–6, 50–1, 54–5, 58–9, 62–3, 65–74 *passim*

**R**
Reid, M. A., 23
research, xiv, 4, 6, 19, 20–1, 31, 37, 42, 45, 46, 48, 50, 54, 56–7, 70, 87
  indicating sources, 8
  practical, 24
  timely start to, 9, 37
  types of, 8–9

revision, 13–28
Reynolds, J., 23

**S**
Scarbrough, H., 23
Section A, 9–10, 17, 19, 22, 35,
    51, 43–53, 85
Section B, 10, 17, 41, 42, 43,
    51–81, 85
Shine, 3, 9, 90
Sloman, M., 23, 66, 72
Stewart, J., 8, 23, 27, 56
*Strategic human resource
    development*, 18, 27
strategic thinking/awareness, 4,
    18, 22–3, 32–5, 59, 68
strategy, 33–4, 35, 47, 50, 57, 59,
    66–7, 68, 71, 75
Swan, J., 23
Swart, J., 23
systematic training
    model/cycle, 23, 67, 72–3

**T**
Tansley, C., 56

thinking performer, xi, xiii, 4,
    11, 16, 20, 26, 30, 35–6, 43,
    56, 65, 70
trade unions, 31, 54, 55–6, 79
    councils, 31
*Training and Development survey*,
    18
*Training in the knowledge
    economy*, 56

**V**
value-added/adding, 17, 19,
    34, 45–6, 48, 64, 70
vision, organisational, 15, 21,
    22, 47
vocational educational
    initiatives (VET), 54–6

**W**
Walton, J., 18, 27
Wilkinson, A., 23
workplace learning, 52, 76,
    78–9

# NOTES